Foreword

I am delighted and honoured to have been asked t
Powley's history of London Youth.

As President of the charity, over the many years in.
never ceased to be inspired and impressed by the achievements of the young people who are
involved in London Youth. The network of members has developed over 133 years, since a
group of visionary leaders established the Girls' Club Union and the Federation of London
Working Boys' Clubs and Institutes. The membership now stands at 400 youth organisations,
in every community in London, providing opportunities for young people to be supported and
challenged to become the best they can be.

Many of these organisations have long and proud histories equally as impressive as that of
London Youth, and over the years, increasing numbers of new organisations have also become
part of the network. The breadth and range of support now offered to young people by these
organisations is incredible, and between them they provide much needed opportunities for
young people every day of the year.

Terry Powley deserves the highest praise for his dedication and determination to tell the story
of how this network of members has developed, and to chronicle the origins of how London
Youth evolved. His book illuminates the subsequent development of the organisation and
its members in adapting to the changing economic and social climate. He has brought a new
historical perspective and an intimate knowledge of the organisation to the task, and on behalf
of London Youth, it has been a pleasure to read his personal account of our story.

Young people in London today face many challenges. But they also have opportunities, and so
much potential to take advantage of those opportunities if they have the right support in place.
This book will be a constant reminder of how previous generations have succeeded in providing
that support despite the many challenges and obstacles.

I hope very much that you enjoy reading the story of how London Youth developed and take
inspiration from it to join us on the next phase of our journey into the future.

President of London Youth:

Field Marshal the Lord Guthrie of Craigiebank GCB LVO OBE DL

Acknowledgements

When my tenure as a trustee on the Board of London Youth came to an end in 2011, I was reluctant to sever my links entirely. I had long harboured an aspiration to write its history, and felt that my somewhat unusual experience of being involved in its affairs at the three levels of national, regional and local gave me a useful perspective to undertake the task. At national level, I represented London Youth on the Board of Trustees of the National Association of Clubs for Young People from 2004–2011, and was its Treasurer from 2005–2010; at regional level, I was a trustee of London Youth from 1988–2011, serving as its Deputy Chair in the last year of that period; and at local level I have been involved from 1968 to the present day with the Vallance Youth Club and the Samuel Montagu Youth Centre.

In bringing the task to completion, I am grateful to Davide Rodrigues and Nick Wilkie for responding so positively to the idea of a publication; to Rosie Ferguson and Shivangee Patel for taking up the implementation of the idea to the point of eventual publication; to Peter Hunter and John Spencer for sharing their knowledge of the organisation and giving constant encouragement; to Mark Wakefield for pointing me in the direction of records and reports associated with the London Union of Youth Clubs and its predecessor bodies; to Valerie Elliott, my cousin, who added to the knowledge of Charles Wrench by trawling the electronic archives and who prepared the photographs for inclusion in the text; to my friend, Derek Pedder, for sharing his collection of memorabilia of the Barking Working Lads' Institute; and to my wife, Milena, for her patient tolerance of my preoccupation with this project! I also thank those clubs–Crown and Manor, Devas, St Andrew's and Alford House–which allowed me to draw on their records to illuminate the role of clubs within the overall history of the organisation. The staff of the London Metropolitan Archives were very helpful in retrieving the archives of London Youth and its predecessor bodies to facilitate my researches.

Dr Terry Powley

June 2014

Contents

Page

1. The Era of Philanthropy, the 1880s–the First World War

The commitment of the Victorian pioneers of the new youth organisations of the late Nineteenth Century was to the established values of the existing social and political order, and their mission was to offer the benefits of their background and culture to working class youths. The task of moral improvement was summed up in this affirmation of William Smith, the founder of the Boys' Brigade in 1883:

> *"The purpose must be the promotion of habits of obedience, reverence, discipline, self-respect and all that tends towards true Christian manliness."*

Bunt and Gargrave have described how youth work in its early manifestations 'came to be the voluntary effort of groups of people outside the class and age in need'. Middle and upper class adults saw it as their role to transmit their values to working class young people. They quote the declaration of the St Christopher's Working Boys' Club in London as an illustration of the unqualified ways in which the early pioneers sought to share their models of good behaviour and high standards with their club members:

> *"It is our aim to ourselves mix with them freely, as far as in us lies, the advantage of better education and tone that a happier fortune has bestowed upon us from our circumstances. We believe strongly that the lads can appreciate and will learn for themselves that subtle something which is called 'good form', which is such an important factor among the high classes." ('The Social Education of the Adolescent', Bunt and Gargrave, 1967.)*

The strength of their attachment to 'good form' was equalled only by the conviction that the natural order of things was under threat. The process of industrialisation and the concentration of the masses in large towns and cities led to the fear that the existing social order was endangered. Asa Briggs draws attention to the testimony of Elizabeth Chapman in 1888:

> *"...there was a 'general revolt against authority in all departments of life which is the note of an unsettled, transitional, above all democratic age', seeing in its tone a reflection of the cultural anxieties of the times." ('A Social History of England', Asa Briggs, 1983.)*

Bunt and Gargrave suggest that, within this historical context, the organisers of the first youth clubs and organisations were motivated as much by thoughts of self-preservation as by pangs of conscience and compassion:

> *"This concern was to prevent certain social ills from happening, or to ameliorate their effects if prevention was not possible, rather than to act positively to bring about social change." ('The Politics of Youth Clubs', Bunt and Gargrave, 1980.)*

It is clear from contemporary accounts that the Victorians saw a social threat in the increased recreation, which had become more available to the working classes, if it was not channelled constructively. Much of the drive which motivated the Victorian philanthropists came from an urgent search for a viable counter–attraction to what Maude Stanley called the 'larking folly' of the music hall, street corner or public house. Frank Booton, in his studies of contemporary historical sources, highlights the 'problem of recreation', which the early pioneers of youth work were struggling to stave off:

> *"...with more time for leisure, the average boy was much more at risk from the repertoire of influences that appalled the middle class conscience, the ill–disciplined bawdiness of the cheap music hall, the sensationalist melodrama of the penny theatre, the largely unregulated public house. But the greatest risk was thought to come from one source–the most pervasively influential and insistently criticised of all working class institutions–the indiscriminately brutalising, ordinary day–to–day routines of the street." ('Studies in Social Education, 1860–1890', Frank Booton, 1985.)*

A contemporary observer portrayed the horrors of the street culture in more concrete and graphic terms:

> *"I object to the life in the streets for the young, there is nothing worth doing to be done there, not even pitch–and–toss. The flaming lights of the corner 'pub', the smell of the fried–fish shop, the discordant yells of street vendors, and the general outrages of their elders require some antidote to be provided for the young." ('An Eton Playing Field', E.M.S. Pilkington, 1896.)*

The antidote was to be found in the virtues of improvement and elevation which young people were to gain from their membership of youth clubs and organisations. This insistence on the need for moral improvement reflected a certainty that the character of young people was deficient and that the values proclaimed by the founders of the new clubs were inherently superior to the values of those who were invited to join. Sweatman, quoted by Frank Booton, was one convinced advocate of the improvement and elevation theme:

> *"The great peril of the system which releases boys at so early an age from the discipline of the school, and turns them out loose upon the world imperfectly taught and trained, is that they are likely to degenerate into very low condition, mental and moral, and gradually to slip away from all improving and elevating influences." ('Studies in Social Education, 1860–1890', Frank Booton, 1985.)*

It was against this background of philanthropy that the origins and inheritance of the Federation of London Working Boys' Clubs and Institutes can be traced. Its first meeting was held in Northumberland Chambers on 10 April 1888. Though this is the first formal record of the Federation's establishment (and W. McG. Eagar in his seminal book, 'Making Men', clearly regards 1888 as the year in which the Federation 'was formed'), the organisation has always taken 1887 as its year of origin. This may indicate that the initial explorations to found the organisation, and the first steps taken to set it up, took place in 1887. W.McG Eagar traces a boys' club back to 1858, when Charles Baker began a club for boys in Bayswater. He considers the Cyprus Boys' Club, formed in 1872, as the first boys' club, in that 'it is recognisable as such by present–day standards and plainly to be named'. That designation, however, is challenged by the St Andrew's Home and Club for Working Boys, which started its work in the Westminster area in 1866 (it began as a home for 'orphans and other lads between the ages of 12 and 18'; it then provided an evening club for these residents; and in 1878 extended the club to the boys of the immediate neighbourhood).

The prime movers of the process that led to the formation of the Federation included Billy Carter, the first missioner of the Eton Mission; T.W.H.Pelham, who ran a boys' club in Long Acre (Pelham was also actively involved in the London Playing Fields Society, formed in 1890, the Regent Street Poly and the Borstall Association); and the Rev. James Denison of St John the Divine, Kennington. In the 1880s, there is evidence that the new boys' clubs were beginning to develop closer links. In February 1886, for example, the St Andrew's Home and Club singing class gave a performance to the club connected with Eton Mission in Hackney Wick, prompted by E.M.S.Pilkington's involvement in both clubs. Such links argued the case for bringing together the various clubs scattered across London in inter–club competitions.

At a subsequent meeting held on 18 October 1888, the Hon T W H Pelham was elected as Chairman. Pelham helped to shape the future direction of the new organisation in writing the 'Handbook to Youth Institutes and Working Boys' Clubs', published in 1889. Dean Farrar wrote a preface, in which he described working boys as the most neglected class of the community:

> *"The youth of both sexes–that vast multitude of boys and girls for whose education millions have been spent by the State and by voluntary exertion–are yearly turned loose, without aid, without sympathy, without exercise, without amusement, into the burning, fiery furnace of the streets of our growing and densely crowded cities. The State does nothing for them, the Church has hitherto done but little, and the chief endeavours to help the young have been due to private endeavour. And it has been pointed out for many years that it is between the ages of 13 and 20 that the final habits of life are mainly formed and it is exclusively at this period of life that a criminal career is either avoided or begun."*

In the handbook, Pelham expressed his preference for 'small, local Institutes, which should never be allowed to outgrow the personal influence of the workers'. He offered advice on the management of boys' clubs, arguing that sport and concerts should be run by a committee chosen from members. Though they would require firm guidance, he felt that gradually more important affairs, such as the election of new members and the management of the club, could be delegated to the boys' committee.

The first public gathering of the new organisation took place on 13 October 1888 at St Andrew's Home and Club, when St Andrew's was presented with the first Federation Cricket Challenge Cup (the club had beaten Harrow Mission by three runs in a close encounter at Lord's on 8 September). It had been hoped that Alfred Lyttelton (the Federation's first President, he was the first person to represent England at both cricket and football and was also Secretary of State for the Colonies from 1903 to 1905) would have been able to take the chair at the presentation, but he was in Ireland at the time.

The Rev. Billy Carter took the chair instead, and used the opportunity to explain the intentions of the founders of the new Federation, as reported in The Chronicle, the monthly record of St Andrew's Home and Club:

> *"The name Federation was rather a long word and not easy to be understood, there had been differences of opinion as to what the amalgamation of the Clubs should be called, some thought union a good term; but it was feared in these days that may look like savouring of politics, and they all wished to keep clear of politics. Then Union had a smack of !! well, a place most of them would like to keep clear of (laughter), so Federation was chosen as the best name to drop on."*

The first annual report of 1890 presented a model of boys' clubs, in which they 'could be in some degree to the poor what the public schools and universities have been to the rich'. Neumann, another recorder and practitioner of the period (he opened a club in the hall of the New College Chapel in north–west London in 1887), was quite clear in his view that boys' clubs should reflect the moral values which he associated with the public schools:

> *"If we look upon it (the club) as an educational enterprise of almost incalculable importance, we shall recognise that the first condition of success is to make it something that is in advance of what the average boy would risk and plan. In this last case, the model will be not a municipal ward, or a limited company with an astute directorate, but a public school or college." ('The Boys' Club', B.Paul Neuman, 1900.)*

28 clubs/institutes joined the Federation in its first full year of operation, and members paid a subscription of one penny a week. Arthur Baxter, closely associated with the Devas Institute in Battersea, became the first secretary of the Federation and remained so until 1891. During these early years, much of the administration of the Federation was carried out by residents of Oxford House, the university settlement founded in 1884 in Bethnal Green.

The organisation immediately set the pattern of its future development by deciding that it would focus on competitive activities between its member clubs. The Council agreed that competitions in the next year would comprise chess, draughts, gymnastics and athletics as well as the popular and traditional games of football and cricket. The consistent enforcement of rules became an urgent issue and a continuing concern of the Council. One club was disqualified from the football league because of an infringement of the age limits, leading the Council to pronounce:

> *"We wish to impress upon managers the necessity of taking every precaution to see that the rule with regard to age is strictly and scrupulously adhered to. Where there is the least doubt as to the age of a lad, the evidence of a birth certificate or an entry in a family bible should be required."*

A similar dispute over umpiring in a cricket match in August 1888 precipitated a further declaration:

> *"It is of the utmost importance that a manager should umpire for each side; if this should be quite impossible, the manager is requested to appoint as umpire some well qualified person not under 25 years of age."*

Problems of this kind prompted the Council to produce a compilation of rules for tournaments, so that there was greater consistency in the management and supervision of the games. The rules were printed in 'The Boys Club Chronicle', the first Federation magazine. The chronicle was published monthly at a cost of a halfpenny. It was used as a channel of communication between member clubs, but also as a way of informing other clubs of the advantages of joining the Federation.

It is clear that, at this early stage of its development, the Federation was mainly a focus for inter–club competitions, as W.McG. Eagar emphasises:

> *"For many years it was little more than an organising centre for competitions, mainly, but not exclusively, athletic. It put virile games for London working boys on a Public School basis, providing umpires and referees, insisting on bona–fide membership of club representatives and on strict observance of age limits. Its ethics of sportsmanship influenced tens of thousands of boys. Its insistence on 'room to play' compelled public authorities to recognise their obligation to manly youth. It regularised all the games and sports dear to young Londoners and made others popular." ('Making Men', W.McG. Eagar, 1953.)*

The Federation's priority at this time was to seek to extend these opportunities to as many boys' clubs as possible.

The challenge of consolidating and expanding the Federation soon gave rise to two familiar problems of growing organisations in general, and the Federation in particular: its name and its financial stability. As early as October 1888, it was suggested that the name of the Federation should be changed from the Federation of London Working Boys' Clubs to the London Federation of London Working Lads, on the grounds that the members of clubs regarded themselves as too old to be called 'boys'. It was decided, however, that no change should be made (the 'and Institutes' part of the original name had already dropped out of general usage, though the Barking Working Lads' Institute was still in existence in 1898–99, when it played in the Federation's football leagues). On the financial front, the examination of the Federation's balance sheet at a Council meeting in October 1890 came to the conclusion that revenue, then solely dependent on subscriptions and private donations, was insufficient to sustain the organisation. It was resolved to institute an appeal for funds. As a result, six supporters guaranteed to donate £5 each (the equivalent of about £540 today) for the years 1892 and 1893. This income gave the Federation sufficient security to reject a proposal to raise the annual subscription for members from 5 shillings to £1. The financial situation improved to such an extent that the organisation reported a balance in hand of £8 (roughly the equivalent of £880 today) in 1897. This improvement did not lead to complacency, however, as shown by the Federation Secretary's suggestion that additional activities should be introduced to arouse the enthusiasm of members. One proposal was that social evenings should be held in each division in order to bring members into closer touch; another was that a Games championship should be held in each club.

The Federation, despite its growing pains, was gradually extending its reach. When the Federation held its annual meeting to distribute prizes on 14 November 1894 at St Andrew's Home and Club, the participants included representatives from Harrow Mission, Kensington

Boys' Club, Willis Street Boys' Club, the Webbe Institute and the Junior Polytechnic. By October 1901, 35 clubs had signed up as members of the Federation, with another six expressing interest, representing a membership of 2,769 boys. Among the participating clubs at this stage were Oxford House, the Brady Club, West Central Jewish, Stepney Jewish, the Webbe, Fairbairn House, Repton, the Devas Institute and St Andrew's. The early clubs to affiliate reflected the seminal influence of the public schools and the universities in establishing the tradition of boys' clubs in London. The Harrow Mission, set up by Harrow School, established a boys' club in the Notting Dale area of London in 1883. The Webbe Institute, which opened in 1888, was the boys' club linked to Oxford House in Bethnal Green, itself associated with Keble College, Oxford (the facilities of the Webbe were to include a Penny Bank and a Sick Club). The Repton Boys' Club was founded in 1884 by Repton School with the support of Oxford House, and remains in existence to this day, acquiring a reputation nationally and internationally as the 'home of boxing' (the Repton Club was set up deliberately 'to touch the lower class of boys than the Webbe Institute'). Fairbairn House in Canning Town started up in 1892 and was the youth section of the settlement, Mansfield House, connected with Mansfield College, Oxford. The Devas Institute had close associations with University College, Oxford, though it was not directly founded by the college. It was established in 1884 by Jocelyn Devas, a graduate of the college, who hired a room over a tavern in Battersea to provide a 'wholesome alternative to the streets and the public house' for working boys. In 1885, he died from a fall while climbing in the mountains of the Swiss Alps, as this report in The Graphic, an illustrated weekly newspaper, outlined:

> "A young Englishman, Jocelyn Devas, recently when strolling with a friend towards the Riffel House from the Gorner Glacier by the Theodule Pass, tried to make a short cut across some wet and slippery rocks whence he could neither advance nor retreat, and as his friend was coming to his aid Mr Devas lost his footing, and slipped down 70 ft on to a ledge of turf, whence he rebounded to some further 70 ft below. When rescued he was found with a fractured skull, and remained unconscious until his death next day."

In his memory, his father offered a substantial endowment, if friends of his son, also graduates of University College, Oxford, would carry on his work.

One development independent of any public school or university support was the foundation of Alford House in Lambeth in 1884. Frank Briant, a young man living in Brixton, took his own initiative to set up a meeting place for boys to cater for their recreational and training needs. He was later elected to both the Lambeth Borough Council and the London County Council, and became the Liberal MP for Vauxhall in 1918. The formation of the Jewish clubs–the Brady Club, Stepney Jewish and West Central Jewish–stemmed from similar philanthropic impulses and moral influences:

> "They were shaped by the long established, often aristocratic, Jews who at the turn of the century found themselves faced with mass and working–class immigration from eastern Europe. For them the task was to Anglicise the newcomers–to convert 'the narrow chested, round–shouldered, slouching son of the Ghetto' into 'an erect and self–respecting man.'" ('From Voluntaryism to Welfare State: A History of the Youth Service in England' Vol 1, Bernard Davies, 1999.)

There were some, also, who saw the influence of boys' clubs, nurtured by the public school ethos, extending beyond London to encompass Imperial expansion at a time of strife in South Africa and the Sudan. The second Earl of Selborne (who was First Lord of the Admiralty from 1900 to 1905) laid this responsibility on the members of St Andrew's Home and Club in addressing the St Andrew's Festival in 1898:

> "I am very happy to be able once again to congratulate the Home and Club on a successful year passed through. Also I think it must be a great pleasure to us all, from the evidence we have heard tonight, to feel how wide is the influence of St Andrew's Home and Club. We have made ourselves felt in Khartoum. It only shows how, with any institution like this, of English boys, it is perfectly certain that the influence of it will go over all the world. You can't keep the English race at home, and therefore it is of the greatest possible consequence that the influence they take with them should be a good influence, and not a bad one. In that respect there is of course a great responsibility upon us, for the people all over the world cannot come to England, and they must therefore judge of the English nation by the Englishmen they see, and any English, or rather British boy or man who goes abroad has a responsibility resting upon him— that he is true to his country and to his religion, and that he carries with him untarnished the good name and good fame of an Englishman, and the honour of a Christian."

Financing the organisation continued to present a problem. Another deficit was reported in May 1902, and the Council agreed that only external help or increased subscriptions from affiliated clubs could reverse this trend. It proved more difficult, however, to reach an agreement on increasing the subscription from clubs. The Hon. Secretary (E.M.S.Pilkington, who was closely involved both with St Andrew's Home and Club and Eton Mission) expressed his frustration in these discussions that, during the time that he had acted as secretary, the Council had rejected every proposal to put the Federation on a sounder financial footing. It was finally agreed in October 1903 that each affiliated club should pay half yearly a capitation fee of one penny per member, provided that the annual subscription payable should in no case amount to a lesser sum than 7 shillings and sixpence (an increase from the existing 5 shillings).

Nevertheless, the financial position remained precarious. In January 1905, it was reported that a sum of £43 would need to be raised if the Federation was to be able to survive until the end of the summer. An appeal for funds evoked little response, but seven members of the Council averted an immediate crisis by undertaking to give or collect £1 by the summer. The financial statement of 1904–05 presented a balance of £2–12–7, which was carried over into the 1905–06 financial year, thus safeguarding the Federation's immediate future.

These financial uncertainties did not prevent the Federation from extending its activities. By 1906, reading, recitation and freehand drawing had been added to the range of activities on offer. In 1907, an Essay competition was introduced. The first topic was: 'Is professionalism harmful to sport?' The topics over the succeeding years tended to be either on national issues or on subjects of relevance to the conduct or development of boys' clubs. In the first category, themes included: 'Ought there to be compulsory military training in England?' (debated in 1910, when the real threat of war was looming); 'Gambling'; 'Should the school leaving age be altered?'; and 'How the

British Empire will be affected by the war' (this coincided with the outbreak of the First World War in 1914). In the second category, subjects covered 'How to get work and how to keep it' and 'How a boys' club should be conducted'. The latter theme was a recurring one for exploration, evoking these comments from one judge, the Head of Cambridge House:

> *"Four of the essays are distinctly good, two of them excellent... I would mark with approval the spirit which is found in every essay that the whole life of the club is educational. The boys appreciate fully the importance of character and the value of the club in forming it."*

It is clear from these topics that the Federation made every attempt to interest its members in relevant and controversial issues.

At the same time, the traditional sporting activities were proving so popular that the Federation was able to use prestigious venues, helped presumably by its influential contacts. In 1906, Stamford Bridge, the home of Chelsea Football Club, accommodated the annual athletics event. In 1910, the cricket finals were played at Lord's, the home of cricket. In 1911, the senior football final was played at Loftus Road (then the ground of Shepherd Bush F.C., now the ground of Queen's Park Rangers). It is doubtful, however, if the standard of play matched the glamour of the venues. A reference to the cricket final at Lord's in the minutes of the Executive Committee contains this cryptic comment:

> *"The form shown by the boys is naturally not of a very high order, and many of our boys would welcome the assistance of good cricketers who would do a little coaching."*

The extent and success of the Federation's sporting activities is reflected in the number of its affiliations to regional and national bodies: in 1910, it was affiliated to the AAA, the Southern Counties Amateur Swimming Association, the Royal Life Saving Society, the Amateur Boxing Association, the Amateur Diving Association and the London Football Association. In the latter case, the boys' clubs were an important influence in the spread of the appeal of football from the public schools to the working classes. There is some evidence to suggest that in the 1870s and 1880s there were few teams that catered for young people. George Biddulph of the St Andrew's Home and Club, for example, is recorded as having had great difficulty in arranging matches for his club's football teams, but this changed as the Fed increased the number and variety of its competitions. Colm Kerrigan, in his history of schoolboy football, underlines the role of boys' clubs in extending the attraction of football to working class young people:

> *"This belief in the practical value of games, as well as the commitment to the public school games ethos, ensured that the teams transmitted the essential elements of association football and its accompanying ideology from the public school to a section of lower-middle-class and working-class youths of London."*
> *('Teachers and Football: Schoolboy Association Football in England, 1885–1915', Colm Kerrigan, 2004.)*

There is some evidence that the degree of emphasis on sporting activities and competitions determined the composition of club membership, as W.McG. Eagar remarks in his book, 'Making Men':

"Comparatively large clubs, like Eton Manor (palatial premises, extensive playing fields and a membership of 400) and Fairbairn House in West Ham, under the aegis of Mansfield House (Free Church), elaborated their programmes at the cost of alienating the poorest and toughest of boys. Such clubs as the Rugby Boys' Club and the Oxford and Bermondsey Clubs (Gordon, Canterbury, Decima Street and Dockhead) persisted in serving the boys from the poorest homes in their area. They made no impression in the Fed competitions, but that degree of failure did not change their objective." ('Making Men', W.McG. Eagar, 1953.)

The more successful clubs progressed to take part in the football leagues organised by the London FA, as well as participating in the Fed's own competitions. A fixture list of the Barking Working Lads' Institute for the 1898–99 season shows that it was competing against clubs, such as the Webbe Institute, Repton, Eton Mission and Fairbairn House, in the Leyton and District League in addition to Federation competitions.

At this time of expanding activities, the number of affiliated clubs within the Federation had risen to 37 by 1910, providing clubs for over 3,000 working boys. These clubs included five parish clubs, six Jewish clubs (the Brady in Spitalfields had been the first to join in 1898), and 11 of public school, university or settlement origin. Cambridge University Mission, founded in 1907, was the idea of a group of Cambridge evangelicals, associated with Ridley Hall, an Anglican theological college. Though Eton College had run a mission in Hackney Wick from the 1880s, its boys' club, the Eton Manor Boys' Club, was formed in 1909. (Though the club was closed in 1967, its name lives on in the form of the Eton Manor F.C., which plays in the Essex Senior League, and in the redevelopment of 'Eton Manor', on the site of its old playing fields adjacent to the main 2012 Olympics grounds, as the base for the Wheelchair Tennis competition in the Paralympic Games and in the future as a tennis, hockey and football centre for local and regional communities.) Reflecting on this 'gratifying progress', the Executive Committee in its report for 1910–11 stated:

"There would seem to be no longer any necessity to defend the utility of Boys' Clubs. There is so much testimony in their favour that their case may be taken as granted. Put in a few words, the object of a Boys' Club is to instil into the boys of the working class that spirit which is the chief characteristic of our English Public Schools."

FIXTURES, 1898-9.

DATE.	CLUB.	GROUND.	RESULT.	GOALS. FOR.	AGST.
Sep. 10	Willis Street	Temple Mills ...		3	0
,, 24	G. E. R. Wagon Works .	Barking	,,	16	0
Oct. 1	*Leyton St. Mary's ...	Leyton	,,	11	0
,, 8	*Walthamstow Excelsiors	Barking	,,	4	0
,, 15	†Webbe Institute ...	Walthamstow... ...	,,	2	0
,, 15	Old Rutlanders ˙ ...	Hackney	,,	5	0
,, 22	*Leyton Mayville ...	Barking	,, ·	16	0
,, 29	*Leytonstone Aylmer ...	Wanstead	,,	1	0
Nov. 5	†Repton	Barking	,,	2	1
,, 5		Away . Scratched ·			
,, 12	*Walthamstow Excelsiors	Walthamstow... ...	,, ·	4	0
,, 19	*Leytonstone Ashville ...	Leytonstone		5	1
,, 26	†ton Mission ...	Hackney ...		1	0
,, 26	Plaistow United ...	Plaistow Scratched			
Dec. 3	*Leytonstone Clairmont .	Barking	~	6	0
,, 10	*Glendale	Wanstead	﹨	5	0
,, 17	†Fairbairn House ˙ ...	Barking			
,, 24	*Walthamstow Holborn Minors	Barking	,,	3	1
,, 26	*Walthamstow Elmsdale	Barking · ...	,,	3	0
,, 31	†Repton	Hackney			
,, 31		Away		0	1
Jan. 7	*Leyton Mayville ...	Leyton		2	0
,, 14	South Woodford Res. ...	Barking	~		
,, 21	*Leytonstone Ashville ...	Barking		1	0
,, 28	†Eton Mission	Barking			
,, 28		Away			
Feb. 4	*Walthamstow Elmsdale	Walthamstow. ...			
,, 11	*Leyton St. Mary's ...	Barking			
,, 18	†Fairbairn House ...	Custom House ...			
,, 18		Away			
,, 25	*Leytonstone Aylmer ...	Barking			
Mar. 4	*Leytonstone Clairmont .	Wanstead			
,, 11	*Walthamstow Holborn Minors	Walthamstow... ...			
,, 18	East Ham United Res.	East Ham ...			
,, 25	*Glendale	Barking			
April 1		Away			
,, 8	†Webbe Institute	Barking			
,, 15	Rainham	Rainham			
,, 22		Barking			

Barking WLI's fixture list, 1898-99

The Federation's confidence in its increasing impact led it to begin to exert its influence in contributing to the national debate on social and educational policy. Though the model of the public school remained dominant, this did not prevent the organisation from making its views known on contemporary measures to improve the health, educational and employment prospects of its members. In May 1901, it joined the Twentieth Century League, which had been formed 'to repair the neglect into which many matters pertaining to the health and upbringing of the youthful and poorer portion of the community in the Metropolitan area has fallen'. In July 1904, the Federation advocated the case for evening classes to support school leavers in gaining the skills which would equip them to obtain jobs:

> *"That having regard to the number of boys who are leaving school at the age of 14 and have not acquired the habit of expending their evenings in rational or useful occupation, this meeting of the managers of FLWBC respectfully urge upon the Education Authority of London the need for evening classes in manual work and physical training for boys between the ages of 12 and 14 who are still attending the elementary schools."*

The Federation also supported Labour Bureaux as a way of increasing access to employment opportunities for members. St Andrew's Home and Club had pioneered this approach as early as 1898, as this extract from the club's chronicle reveals:

> *"We propose, though only on a small scale, to open a Labour Bureau at the Home. It sometimes happens that we at the Home hear of places, such as Shorthand or Type-writing Clerkships, Caretakers' places, &c, &c, which might be suitable for Old Boys, but which are lost owing to our not knowing at the moment who are in need of places of those descriptions.*
>
> *On the other hand, some of the Old Boys may sometimes hear of places, especially good openings for learning a trade, which might be useful for some of the present Boys in the Home and Club."*

In October 1905, the Hon. Secretary argued for a closer link between boys' clubs and elementary schools to mutual advantage. He suggested that club managers and teachers should co-operate in persuading boys to attend evening classes after they left school. The Federation agreed to take more initiative itself in arranging lectures at clubs.

Its grappling with new legislation which affected club members prompted the Federation to convene a special meeting to discuss the newly introduced national insurance measures. The Council passed this resolution:

> *"That this meeting of the Council of the FLWBC, after a full discussion as to the best methods which they could advise their boys to adopt with regard to insurance under the act, recommend the managers of constituent clubs to join some good approved society."*

The measures to provide insurance against sickness and unemployment were part of a programme of social reform set in motion by the Liberal government elected in 1906, of which the Federation was supportive, including the introduction of medical inspections in state schools. Many of the legislative changes stemmed from the impact of a spate of influential reports on health, juvenile unemployment, health and medical inspection. This programme in some ways marked the beginning of a shift away from charitable voluntaryism to State intervention, as W.McG. Eagar traces:

> "Between 1904 and 1914, the inadequacy of voluntaryism in the social work sphere became more obvious to thoughtful observers. Social-economic changes reduced the number of men who could afford to engage themselves whole-time, for a few years at any rate, in unpaid social work. Doctrines of salvation by State action rather than by personal service permeated the minds of younger men who, in the previous generation, might have joined crusaders in the East-end, battling against the consequences of poverty." ('Making Men', W.McG. Eagar, 1953.)

Yet the Federation's forward-looking stance on these matters of national debate was not always a feature of its internal discussions. In April 1906, its cohesiveness was disturbed by an attempt to remove Jewish clubs from membership. The proposer of the motion based his case on three issues: Jewish clubs had 'great advantage over others in matters of management'; their members were 'often above the rest in age and social position'; and some other members had 'a prejudice against mixing with Jewish lads'. Another speaker contended that the Federation should be doing more to promote Christianity, and he 'did not see how this could be done as long as both Jew and gentile clubs were affiliated'. There was a general view that the Federation should not lose the help and co-operation of the Jewish clubs, and a motion 'that the feeling of this meeting is that the Jewish clubs remain in the Federation' was passed by seven votes to six (the managers of Jewish clubs themselves refrained from voting).

Another section of the community was targeted as a harmful influence on the male members of clubs. The clubs had always been limited to boys, but some managers nonetheless took further steps to insulate boys from what they saw as the negative influence of girls. The manager of the Eton Manor Boys' Club initiated a debate in 1912 on how boys aged between 14 and 18 could be separated from the company of girls. He had formed a Junior Bachelor Society in his club, which attracted 40 of the total membership of 120. Members were asked to sign a form in which they promised not to 'walk about with girls' until they reached the age of 18: 'if a boy broke this rule, he was tried by the other members of the society, and punished according to the heinousness of the crime'. Unsurprisingly, other speakers said that they thought that the influence of girls was beneficial and should be encouraged under 'proper conditions'. Even when speakers agreed that girls were the major factor in keeping boys away from clubs, they were alarmed at the prospect of having to start a Junior Bachelor Society to counteract their influence! At a later discussion, 'picture theatres' were cited as another attraction which stood in the way of boys regularly attending their clubs.

Dissension of this kind did not slow down the consolidation of the Federation's work. A more stable financial position allowed the Federation to consider an offer from the Council of Social Institutes in April 1907 to share its office at the W.H. Smith Memorial Hall in Portugal Street at an annual rent of £26. This sum also included the services of a clerk for one hour a day.

These arrangements only lasted until 1910, when Charles Wrench began his long period of distinguished service with the Federation:

> *"In accepting the dual role of Hon. Secretary and Treasurer, Mr Wrench desired it to be distinctly understood that he could not carry on the work under the circumstances existing at the Smith Memorial Hall where he considered the office accommodation unequal to the needs of the Social Institutes Union and the Fed."*

A sub–committee was set up to search for a separate office for the work of the Federation at a rental not exceeding £40 per year. The Secretary was able to report in October 1910 that a new office had been found at Bridge House (a name that was to recur in later years in the organisation's history!), 10 Victoria Street at a rental of £35 per year. Extra charges for utilities and cleaning would bring the total cost to £40 (roughly the equivalent of £4,000 today). These additional commitments meant that the Federation suffered a deficit of £32 in 1912. It still relied mainly on the financial support of a number of individuals closely associated with the organisation, though it received in that year a grant of £10 from the Worshipful Company of Grocers, the first recorded donation from a city livery company.

The formal opening of the new office took place on 17 November 1910, when a portrait of HRH Prince Arthur of Connaught, painted and presented by Mr de l'Hopital, was unveiled. Prince Arthur, the grandson of Queen Victoria, had become the Federation's first Patron in 1904 and had taken an active part in the organisation's fundraising efforts. He made his own donation of £5 to the Federation in January 1914. The St Andrew's Home and Club records show that Mr de l'Hopital was also teaching drawing classes at the club in 1910.

The search for premises was soon followed by an examination of the case for paid clerical assistance. This issue had first been raised by E.M.S Pilkington in 1901 when he argued for the establishment of a 'regular' office, with 'proper' clerical help, not just to deal with the increasing administration but also to make the Federation better known to potential members and the general public. In May 1912, the Hon. Secretary returned to the issue by pointing out that the detailed work in running the Federation's affairs was becoming increasingly arduous. (Even at this stage in the Federation's development, the job must have been a demanding one on top of his full time work as a businessman.) It was imperative in his view to obtain the services of a paid secretary. By the end of the year, T.O Williams had been appointed as secretary at a salary of £25 per year, the organisation's first paid employee. The rationale for a paid assistant was not just to relieve Charles Wrench of clerical duties, but also to allow him to devote more time to 'the all–important and indispensable work of club visiting'.

Much of the impetus behind the early developments of youth organisations sprang from deep–seated feelings that working class young people should be introduced to the values and mores of the upper and middle classes. But there is less attention in the literature of the times about how the young people themselves regarded the aims and motivation of the club founders and managers. The fact that the boys' clubs were successful suggests that most members bought into the values and approved of the offer of the club. Others may have adapted what the clubs had to offer to their own requirements for physical activity, particularly football and other organised games, and social interaction, without any particular regard to those underlying values and motivations.

Yet others strived to assert a common humanity that obliterated class differences: the Harrow Club declared that 'it is not the mixing of 'classes' that is needed, but the oblivion of class, if only for one hour in the week, in the light of a common humanity'; similarly, the Oxford and Bermondsey Club stated that 'the OBC was no longer Oxford's effort to save Bermondsey, but a fraternal association of Oxford men with Bermondsey men and men–to–be, which had completely overcome barriers of class and education'. Certainly, many of the philanthropists transcended class differences, developing an understanding and rapport with club members, and gaining insights into the conditions of life of deprived communities. W.MG.Eagar makes the point that the founders and supporters of clubs learned much from their deepening knowledge of working class communities and used that knowledge to add their voice to social change:

> *"Boys' Club men made a notable contribution to the knowledge which broke down the complacent views of Early Victorian times that poverty was inevitable and the proper lot of those who did not rise above it...In the long term their great achievement was to bring home to the mind and conscience of the nation that it should do comprehensively and methodically what they were doing experimentally and partially." ('Making Men', W.McG.Eagar, 1953.)*

Of course, the accounts of the early years of youth clubs represent the recorded history of the youth work in its organised form during this period. There may also have been an unrecorded, hidden history built on working class patterns of organisation which put a higher value on co–operative, participatory forms of youth work:

> *"What we do not know is whether the articulated, recorded and published statements of the 'Smiths, Baden Powells, and Pelhams', which led to the formation of national organisations, were the sum total of initiatives by individuals for young people. If the working class was capable of sponsoring insurance societies, co–operatives and working men's clubs, then it is also possible that they engaged in localised and spontaneous youth work. If it took place, however, it has not yet been recorded." ('Young People, the Youth Service and Youth Provision', National Youth Bureau, 1981.)*

2. The Era of Citizenship, 1914–the Second World War

The philanthropic values of the late Nineteenth Century persisted into the early Twentieth Century, but the impact of the First World War and the franchise reforms which succeeded it moderated to some extent their dominance and quickened democratic impulses. The extension of the vote to all men over 21 who satisfied a six months' residence qualification helped to create a climate in which boys could be perceived as being more independent. A.J.P. Taylor declared that 'war smoothed the way for democracy', and it is evident in the writings of the times that the club was increasingly seen as a training ground for citizenship for a wider section of the community, rather than just as a setting in which public school schemes of 'esprit de corps' could be transmitted to a working class audience.

This sense of a new order of democracy, which needed to be trained in the art of government, is conveyed in the writings of C.E.B. Russell, whose book, 'Working Class Lads' was a very influential textbook, first published in 1908 and revised by his widow in 1932. Russell also asserted considerable sway over the development of youth work by chairing the Juvenile Organisations Committee, set up in 1916 to give a firmer direction to work with young people. He put forward a concept of youth work as 'fitness for citizenship' and for manhood:

> "It will probably have struck some of our readers that many of the results which
> we claim for boys' clubs are precisely those which have made our public schools
> the special pride of the country. The significance of this in relation to the nation
> may be appreciated when we reflect that if our rulers in the Nineteenth Century
> were educated at Eton, our rulers in the Twentieth Century are being educated
> in the elementary schools. If it is largely the public school spirit which has made
> England great in the past, any means by which a similar spirit may be fostered
> in the boys who leave the elementary schools at the very age when the sons of
> the monied classes are entering on the most vulnerable years of their school life
> is of incalculable importance." ('Lads' Clubs: Their History, Organisation and
> Management', C.E.B. Russell,1932.)

The growth of the Federation was arrested by the outbreak of the First World War. Out of a membership of 43 clubs in 1914, nine clubs closed due to the immediate impact of the war on their operations. Most of the Fed's competitions continued to take place, but the number of entries was much smaller than usual, especially in the senior competitions. It was clear that the Federation was finding it difficult to maintain its work, as more and more managers and committee members were called away on military service. Six members of the Executive Committee were serving in France, two clergymen were Army Chaplains; and the Hon. Treasurer was an interpreter at the Prisoners of War Camp in Jersey. The Head of the Trinity College, Oxford Mission in Stratford, Tom Allen, was killed at the front in February 1915:

> "He was responsible for starting and managing the boys' clubs, Christchurch
> and Oxford Trinity. At the beginning of the war, he enlisted as a private in the
> Grenadier Guards, but shortly afterwards accepted a commission in the Irish
> Guards, and was in training with them at Warley for some months. He went out

*to France with his regiment early in February and was immediately sent up to
the trenches, and after being there for only three weeks he was killed by a shell
which burst on the parapet in front of him."*

The 1913–14 Executive Committee report took some satisfaction that the boys' clubs had
contributed to the 'spirit of patriotism' evoked by the declaration of war:

*"It is a sense of satisfaction to hear how magnificently the past and present
members of the affiliated clubs have responded to the call of their country, a
result which the Committee feel sure is largely due to the excellent training
given in the various clubs which are doing so much to foster the spirit of
patriotism, comradeship and self-denial among the working boys of London."*

The Federation took what steps it could to adapt its activities to the state of war. It introduced
military drill into its physical training competition and decided to base the competition on the
Army handbook, not as previously on the Navy handbook. It was also agreed that refugees from
Belgium should be eligible for Federation competitions during their membership of an affiliated
club. Only one competition was dropped on account of the war, and the active help of senior
members was compensating for the loss of older members and supporters. Football remained
a mainstay and an important vehicle of what the Federation wanted to achieve, as the annual
report for 1912–13 illustrates:

*The Committee are convinced that the Fed is doing most useful work in
teaching the rising generation to play football in the proper spirit and in a
clean sportsmanlike manner; and though the expenses are out of all proportion
to those incurred in connection with the other competitions, they feel the
expenditure is justified. The average working boy thinks and talks about
football more than anything else during the winter months, and it is far better
that he should be taught to play, and play in the right spirit, rather than go and
watch professional matches."*

24 teams competed in the senior league and 12 in the junior division, involving 242 matches.

The Executive Committee saw its continuing work with boys as assisting the war effort:

*"The Committee hopes that during the coming winter all club members who are
under military age will recognise that it is their duty to equip themselves for the
future by greater efforts at their work, their games and their evening classes."*

But the Federation was strict in condemning the increasing willingness of recruiting sergeants
to enlist boys under the age of 18, and in many cases under 16.

It was also alert to the social consequences of the war and the effect of the removal of influential
managers and senior members from the active life of clubs:

*"One of the most important lessons of the past year of war has been the striking
need of a controlling influence amongst the working class boys. The withdrawal
of hundreds and thousands of men from civil life to fill the ranks of the Army
and the Navy has raised the boy worker to a position of unprecedented*

independence and responsibility. At the same time, the absence of parental
control, the darkness of the streets and the spirit of lawlessness and adventure
aroused by the war have caused a remarkable increase of juvenile crime, and
have focused attention on the special problem of the boy worker."

The sense that new social conditions were precipitating new social problems led the Federation
to give more thought and analysis than ever before to the context of its work:

"The first essential that there should be a general recognition that the juvenile
adult period is a special problem requiring its own special treatment and
institutions is slowly being reached, but there is still a tendency to cater in the
same institutions for the school boy and the boy who is at work earning wages."

The Federation also sought, in this changing situation, to capture and define what it saw to
be the essential elements of a successful club. These were seen to include: physical enjoyment
('to absorb a boy's energies and promote physical development'); mental interest (games
of skill, reading, lectures, debates); discipline ('as a condition to both the former'); as far as
possible, self–government by club members; 'a frank, strong recognition of moral and religious
obligations'; and fellowship within the club.

The Federation's conviction that the growing importance of boys' clubs was being increasingly
recognised prompted it in its 1916–17 report to stress the significance of the boys' club within
the hard–pressed circumstances of its members' everyday lives:

"Many of those who read about a boys' club have only a very faint conception of
what it really is. The West End club man regards his club merely as a convenient
place for meeting his friends, and where he can pass his afternoons or evenings.
To the working boy, it is of far greater importance. Many of the boys come from
exceedingly squalid homes, or from homes which are terribly overcrowded.
It is no uncommon thing for a boy to be one of a family of seven or eight, who
live entirely in one or two rooms; the parents are therefore just as anxious as
the boys themselves that they should 'clear out' of the house. The club becomes
the only place where they can spend their evenings in common and pleasant
companionship after a hard day's work. To many of these boys, the club is a
centre of local patriotism, and their ambition in life is as much to become a
credit to it as to promote their own advancement."

These realities of daily life had implications for the role of the club manager:

"The club manager also has to act in a hundred and one different capacities
and has, not infrequently, to advise the boys on legal and medical questions and
on questions of employment; he is frequently consulted by the parents as to their
son's future, and as regards the many problems which arise in the domestic life
of the poor."

Sir Charles Wrench, Secretary 1910–1945

The war conditions, and concerns about the place of juveniles at a time of social flux and change, led to the creation of Juvenile Organisation Committees (JOCs) by the Home Secretary in 1916. The role of the Federation in identifying the issues and seeking a more systematic response is reflected in the appointment of Charles Wrench to the central JOC. Local JOCs were set up in London and all towns of over 20,000 inhabitants in England, Scotland and Wales. They were seen as a way of bringing all organisations into closer touch, and preventing unnecessary overlapping, in the hope that larger numbers of boys and girls would be encouraged to join a youth organisation on leaving school.

The advent of the JOC led to a debate in 1918 about the structure of the Federation. It was felt that the establishment of JOCs at Borough level should be imitated by the Federation as part of a process of decentralisation. In 1919, a sub-committee was set up to consider a number of proposed alterations to the constitution necessitated by the introduction of Borough Federations. It was stipulated that the definition of a 'working boy' was one between the ages of 14 and 18 who had attended a public elementary school; the Federation was to be open to individual working boys' clubs in London and London Borough Federations or Associations of Working Boys' Clubs; clubs affiliated to a Borough Federation could only be represented on the Federation's Council through the official representative of the Borough Federation, though clubs affiliated directly to the Federation would be directly represented on the Council.

Within these new arrangements, individual clubs had to conform to the following conditions: the possession of their own club premises or a regular meeting place; a membership of at least 15; a schedule of a minimum of two meetings a week; a responsible manager; and regular subscriptions to be paid by boys over 14.

The formation of the JOC, as well as prompting changes to the Federation's constitution, was welcomed as a 'happy sign' that the Government was alive to the new issues of the time. The Federation set up a sub-committee to consider what it could do to bring the organisation more in touch with the changes which had been precipitated by the war years. It was also compelled to assess its attitude to the increasing role of the State in youth provision, as exhibited in the establishment of the JOCs. At the AGM in November 1919, one member stated strongly his view that the Federation should not expect, or seek, State aid: 'he hoped that the Committee would not rely on such an unlikely source of income'. The Chairman concluded the discussion by expressing a contrary opinion:

> "That now work among young people was established as work of national importance, and recognised as such by the State, there was every hope that State assistance would be forthcoming."

The Federation also gained from the growing influence of the JOC in shaping the conditions in which boys' clubs could thrive. At a time of continuing financial pressures and shortages, the JOC's Secretary had persuaded the Board of Trade (Coal Mines Department) to issue instructions to its Divisional Officers that they should give sympathetic consideration to reasonable applications to provide fuel for clubs, 'provided that economy is given every consideration'. It also lobbied the Ministry of Transport to give juvenile organisations reduced railway fares in travelling to and from summer camps.

The end of the war, marked by the return of managers and senior members and the restoration of more settled conditions, brought about a revival of activity. Several clubs which had left the Federation during the war rejoined and new ones enrolled.

A Fed circular welcomed the end of the war and anticipated an increased focus on the welfare of young people:

> *"Nothing really matters now the war is over, and there is no more awful fighting, and everyone can look forward to a time of peace and happiness after the years of misery and suffering through which the whole world has been passing. In the near future there is likely to be a tremendous impetus to social work amongst boys and girls, and it is to be the duty of every club member to do all he possibly can for his club, and to induce other boys to join."*

Other social and educational changes had the effect of revitalising the clubs. The introduction of the 48–hour week in so many trades meant that boys could leave work earlier and spend more time in their club. The operation of the new Education Act, which made it compulsory for boys to remain at school until the end of the term in which they reached the age of 14, prompted many clubs to look for ways in which boys could continue their general education at the club.

Despite a surge in attendance, the Federation remained concerned, and not a little disturbed, that clubs were losing boys at the ages of 16 and 17, 'because a chance meeting at a street corner has led to subsequent meetings and a flirtation in the dark alleys and back streets in the neighbourhood of the club'. Yet the Federation, rather than seeking to remove boys from the influence of girls (as the manager of the Eton Manor Boys' Club had proposed in 1912), took the novel step of introducing mixed evenings and dances at clubs, 'so that members may be able to enjoy petticoat society under decent conditions'. The language and the comments in the 1918–19 report betray a lingering ambivalence about allowing girls into clubs, but the Federation saw the mixed evenings as a means of maintaining its 'influence' over its club members.

> *"The subject bristles with difficulties, but the Committee hope that a solution may be found by which clubs may be able to provide their members with opportunities of meeting girls of their own age, and thus retain and strengthen their influence over a larger proportion of their members."*

The 1918–19 annual report asserted the Federation's view that the organisation had become far better known over the previous year. It was recognised by the JOC (now attached to the Board of Education) as the body to which all working boys' clubs should affiliate, either directly or through their Borough Federation. It made recommendations and proposals which 'are more carefully considered by public bodies than would be the case if such recommendations were made by individual clubs'.

The burden of the new organisational requirements led the Council again to consider the need for a paid organising secretary (it seems that the post of secretary, agreed in 1912, had lapsed during the war years). In 1919, F.O Marston was appointed as full–time Secretary, relieving Charles Wrench of all detailed work at headquarters. New, more centrally located premises were obtained at Memorial Hall Buildings near to Ludgate Circus.

The Secretary's salary and the office move accounted for a deficit, and the Federation launched an appeal for funds, its first public one, signed by Prince Arthur of Connaught and Lord Desborough:

> *"The Fed has never previously made a public appeal; it has no funds, and its income of £150, subscribed by a few friends, is totally inadequate to carry on the work. It requires at least £1,000 a year to enable it to assist clubs, which have no support such as is accorded to those backed by the public schools and colleges, to defray the cost of competitions, and to pay a good secretary and office expenses."*

As a result of the appeal, donations increased from £51 to £236 (approximately £10,300 at present values). Yet the Federation, while grateful for the outcome, realised that it was not sufficient to meet its increasing needs, and continued to search for additional income. It was also increasingly conscious of the need for more volunteers:

> *"Reports from the universities show that the need for improvement in social conditions is now widely recognised. Lectures on economics at Oxford and Cambridge are crowded, the LSE is full to overflowing: theorists abound, but where are the practical men?"*

To help cut down on expenditure, the Federation moved to new premises at 1 Bear Lane, Southwark Street. This space was provided rent free by Charles Wrench, who lived there and used it as the centre of his manufacturing business.

By 1920, the Fed claimed 130 affiliated clubs (the pre–war figure was 43) and 3,400 members. The majority of affiliated clubs were based in Bermondsey, St Pancras, Stepney, West Ham and Westminster (the traditional roots of the organisation), but–assisted by the JOC's efforts–clubs were beginning to spring up in Marylebone, Finsbury and Islington. The Fed was particularly keen to attract funding to support the work of such smaller, often fragile, clubs, not just to maintain its regular organising work.

Start of Junior Half-Mile Team Race. Athletic Sports, Stamford Bridge, May 29th, 1920

At the 1920 AGM, the Treasurer offered his view that more financial support should be required of affiliated clubs in the form of increased entrance fees to competitions. He also put forward the idea of a co-operative scheme selling sporting kits and equipment with the profits going to the Federation. The store was launched as 'The Co-operative Sports Supply Association', and in its first year £20 accrued to Federation funds and £25 was carried over as capital in the coming year. But this new source of revenue did not slow down the search for additional ways of strengthening the Federation's financial position. At the 1923 AGM, the Hon. Secretary stressed the necessity of the Fed becoming a much larger and more powerful body in the post-war conditions. Consequently, a letter was sent to The Times to promote the work of the Fed and to appeal for funds. The next AGM received the announcement of an anonymous donation of £250 'with great applause'.

In these years, the Federation continued to look beyond its own boundaries in developing an organisation to represent the boys' club movement nationally. The idea of a national organisation was first mooted in 1921, when the Liverpool Union of Boys' Clubs made the suggestion to the National Council of Social Service. The Federation was prominent in convening a conference at Toynbee Hall, based in Spitalfields and the first of the university settlement houses, in October 1924 to consider in detail the possibility of creating a new organisation:

> *"In the opinion of the Executive Committee, this step is an event in the history of the boys' club movement. Hitherto, with the exception of local Federations in London, Liverpool, Manchester and a few other places, boys' clubs have not been linked together, but it is hoped through the national organisation to eventually bring together all the boys' clubs in the country. Such a union should prove of immense value to the boy life of the country, and will be a means of bringing club managers together for exchange of views and discussion of problems dealing with their particular club."*

In February 1925, the Federation made a grant of £5 towards a national conference to take the idea forward, and in November the National Association of Working Boys' Clubs was formed.

In responses to other areas of national debate, and as part of the drive to apply the concept of an educated society and an informed citizenship, the Federation warmly approved the provisions of the 1921 Education Act, which extended schooling beyond the age of 14 to 8 hours a week (the time coming out of working hours) until the age of 16 was reached. The Fed accepted that educational classes in clubs had failed to reach the majority of members and saw in the new arrangements an opportunity to keep alive the 'habit of learning':

> *"The curriculum is adapted to the needs of the boy who is no longer a child, but is for the better part of the week engaged in earning his living. Physical training takes an important part, and the medical inspection, perfunctory as it is, has in it the germs of a system which should be of incalculable value to the boy in the most crucial years of his physical development."*

In response to these new measures, one affiliated club maintained its own school, and others provided premises for the new day continuation schools. The Federation, while welcoming the partial extension of education, lobbied strenuously to extend it for two full years until the end of the boy's sixteenth year, putting itself at the forefront of social and educational change:

> *"The Committee hopes that the London County Council will at the first opportunity extend the age to 16, and in the meantime will not be restrained by fear of temporary unpopularity from putting into force the compulsory powers which they have been given by the legislation. All measures which have extended the age of general education have been unpopular at first, both with the children themselves and with the parents. It is only after some years of experience that the extension will be universally recognised as a boon both to the individual and to the country."*

Financial difficulties still beset the Federation. The position was described as 'precarious in the extreme' in the 1922–23 report. The Fed had only been saved from bankruptcy in the previous year by the generosity of an anonymous donor, who made a present of some securities which were lodged with the Federation's bankers against a temporary loan of £350 (there is no evidence to substantiate this, but it is reasonable to speculate, given the regularity of his annual donations to the organisation and the occasional loan to support new initiatives, that this may have been Charles Wrench himself). To ease the financial pressures, the Federation sought to diversify its donors beyond the customary individual benefactors. The City Corporation gave a grant of £25; the proprietors of the Daily Telegraph donated £5; and the Most Worshipful The Armourers and Braziers Company gave a donation of 5 guineas. The Co–operative Sports Supply Association (which had been transferred to the Federation's headquarters) now had a turnover of £900 worth of goods (around £46,000 at today's values). The same person, who had handed over the securities, donated £250 in 1923, helping the Federation to declare a surplus of £114 in the 1923–24 financial year.

Notwithstanding the constant anxieties about adequate funding, the Federation was establishing a high reputation in the post–war years. At one level, it continued to promote what it called 'the spirit of sportsmanship' stimulated by its busy schedule of organised competitions, as the Duke of York (later to become King George VI) recognised in his speech at the Boxing Finals in April 1922:

> *"I need not tell you that I think and know that you are all sportsmen in the true sense of the word. From what I have seen at the boxing tonight, you are all sportsmen and gentlemen. You have all learned that most important lesson, how to play for your club and not for yourself. In the boxing, those who have got through the various rounds were all fighting for their club as much as themselves. That is the right kind of spirit and what we want in this old country of ours."*

At another level, the Commissioner of Prisons in his report for 1923–24 concluded that the work of boys' clubs helped to stem the increase in juvenile delinquency due to unemployment:

> *"A brighter side to the picture is the success of those forms of social service which provide education and mental outlook for young persons of both sexes. Even in present circumstances it is rare for a lad or girl to be received into prison who has been a member of a good boys' or girls' club, a boy scout or a girl guide. The voluntary workers in these and similar other organisations are rendering a public service of which the value cannot be overestimated."*

The Federation was confident and clear in its assessment, presented in the 1922–23 annual report, of the value and impact of a boys' club:

"A boys' club has a distinct place in the life of the working boy. On leaving school, he loses the discipline of the school and the influence of the teacher. His home can provide little that he requires, and he is left to choose between the street, with all that it implies, and the club, if club there be. The club is really his home in the evening, and the spirit of the club, and the influence of the manager, become the chief factors in building up the man."

The Federation made attempts to 'build up the man' and help him plan for the future in encouraging clubs to establish a National Savings Association. The National Savings Committee approached the Fed in 1924, in the hope that it would bring its work to the notice of boys' clubs. The national savings movement had been launched during the period of financial duress in 1916 as a means of providing people with small incomes with a safe and attractive investment. It was also a way of obtaining funds to pursue the war effort. The Fed commended the scheme to its affiliated clubs, seeing thrift as part of the character–building process:

"In a boys' club, a Savings Association is especially valuable, inasmuch as it not only helps its members to save and thus prepare for future needs, but tends to develop in them habits of thrift with the resultant valuable effects upon their characters."

The organisation, however, remained immune to the overtures of the National Organisation of Girls' Clubs (NOGC). As long before as 1913, the NOGC had approached the Federation to send a joint deputation to the London County Council (LCC) to press the case for clubs to receive grants if they established drill classes. Again in 1914, the NOGC had written to the Federation to make a joint approach to the Board of Education about access to general grants for youth groups. The Fed replied that, owing to the pressure of other matters, it had not been able to examine the matter in detail. It advised the NOGC to act independently. In April 1924, the NOGC wrote again to ask if the Federation would join in a deputation to the Government to discuss the raising of the school leaving age. The Hon. Secretary was asked to reply in these rather guarded terms, a strange response given the Federation's own unambiguous representations in the wake of the 1921 Education Act:

"Federation opinion on this subject is divided: some favour continued education during the whole 14 to 18 years period, while others wish for the raising of the school leaving age. It is impossible, therefore, to appoint a representative, with a definite mandate from this organisation."

It is interesting that the Federation contacted the NOGC in December 1924 to advise that the question of affiliation between the organisations would have 'to remain in abeyance' because of the probable formation of a national federation of boys' clubs. There is no other reference in the records to the nature of the discussions about affiliation, so it is difficult to be certain of whether there were any real attempts at this stage to forge closer links between these organisations and their respective member clubs.

It was at this time–perhaps to define its profile more clearly but certainly to abbreviate its title and to bring it into line with that of similar organisations in other parts of the country–that the Federation again discussed a change of name. In June 1925, it was proposed that the name should be changed to the London Federation of Boys' Clubs. After much debate, five committee members voted for and five against. The Chairman stated that, while he was in favour of the proposal, he felt that he had 'no alternative but to vote constitutionally, in accordance with usual custom'. He therefore gave his vote against the motion, which was defeated. A decision to change the name was finally agreed in December 1927, taking effect in 1928.

During the 1920s, the Federation strengthened its development along familiar lines. The greater part of agendas continued to focus on competitions, the eligibility of boys to participate and the definition of a working boy (defined in 1926 as 'one between the ages of 14 and 19 who has attended a public elementary school'). The reading competition in 1922 was judged by an official of the Board of Education, who praised the quality of the entries:

> *"To myself, there was much encouragement in the assurance given me by the performance of these lads that the education they had received in the elementary schools (from which, I presume, they were drawn, and with the welfare of which I am so much concerned) has attained to such success in a direction in which it is so often accused of failure."*

The Fed reported on the cricket final, played at the Oval in September 1924:

> *"The final between St Andrew's Home and Club and the Cambridge University Mission (CUM) was played at the Oval on Saturday September 27th. There had been a lot of rain during the week, but Saturday was a brilliant day, and though the wicket was a bit soft, it did not cut up too badly. CUM won the toss and, following the usual Fed fetish, put their opponents in to bat first. St Andrew's seized their opportunity and after a nervous start knocked up 99 runs, mainly through the sturdy hitting of C.Shaw. The bowling of CUM was good, but was changed too frequently to give the respective bowlers a chance.*
>
> *CUM went in to beat this score with just over one hour in which to make the runs, but against the deadly bowling of St Andrew's and the inevitable 'Final' nerves were all out for 10 runs in about half an hour. St Andrew's Home and Club are a useful team, and some of the cricket was remarkably good."*

In 1927, a representative football team played against the Royal Military College, Camberley and Charterhouse School. In the same year, the masters of the city livery companies were invited to attend the boxing finals, inaugurating an association that was to endure thereafter. The Hon. Secretary was asked to write to the MCC to enquire whether the Fed could be given any surplus cricket gear. The MCC replied that, once its cricket equipment was no longer used by the club, it was of no use to anyone!

The organisation's finances during this period were more stable, though in 1925 the Hon. Treasurer reported that liabilities exceeded cash at the bank by £381. The search for new sources of income was therefore unrelenting. He presented a scheme to enlist supporters to subscribe an annual sum of money. This scheme was an ambitious one: a supporter who promised to subscribe a minimum of 5 shillings a year, and to persuade others to enrol, became a Federate; when a Federate had enrolled 12 others, he or she became an Associate; an Associate who enlisted the participation of 30 others became a Fellow; and a Fellow who attracted the support of 60 others became a Companion. Almost immediately, the Federation had gained 60 Federates (existing annual donors were invited to enrol as Federates) and one Associate. The hope was that the scheme would raise a regular income sufficient to cover the organisation's annual expenses. The number of Federates had increased within the year to 600 and, by 1928, to 757. Count Vivian Hollander and Captain Herbert Buckmaster had been so successful in recruiting supporters that they achieved the highest grade of Companion. This new source of income stabilised the financial position to the extent that the 1925–26 annual report could declare:

> "The financial situation may be said to be in hand, and the intention henceforth will be to endeavour to 'cut the coat according to the cloth', and not again be handicapped by a debt."

The annual report of 1925–26 portrayed that year as one of the most successful and eventful in the history of the Federation. The additional income and increasing membership reflected an expansion of interest in the work of the organisation both among subscribers and the clubs. One major event of that year was the General Strike. There is little reference in the records to the impact of that event on the clubs, and it seems that the Federation did not feel that it should, as a voluntary organisation, be drawn into a political controversy which had polarised the nation. It felt more comfortable in seeking reconciliation in the aftermath of the strike and in building bridges between the classes. After the strike had ended, it organised a Camp of Understanding at Maidstone in Kent:

> "The main idea was to get some of the boys away from London into healthy surroundings during this critical time, and to bring them into close personal contact with some public schoolboys at the camp."

The Federation's confidence increased further in 1926–27. 106 clubs were now affiliated, representing a total membership of 7,200 boys. It pursued its ambition to reach out to the 60,000 boys of club age in London who did not belong to a club. It retained the hope that, with any surplus funds, it could take the initiative to form new clubs, set up a training centre for club managers, acquire a sports ground and establish a permanent camping site:

> "This may be somewhat ambitious, but unless the Fed can see well ahead, and anticipate the needs of its clubs, it will not be justifying its existence."

A new Borough Federation was formed in Finsbury. The link with the City livery companies was strengthening: the Clothworkers' Company donated £100 (around £5,320 in today's terms), the Grocers' Company £10 and the Mercers £5. The London Parochial Charities (LPC) gave £50 as its first grant of many. The LPC was a significant donor, in that it was a powerful charity able to give useful and continuing support. The Rt Hon. Lloyd George (Prime Minister from 1916 to 1922) contributed a guinea.

The Camp of Understanding, Maidstone, Whitsun, 1926

The organisation continued to seek donations from wealthy individuals, utilising its links with influential Establishment figures. In April 1928, it was reported that Lord Rothermere, the press magnate and proprietor of the Daily Mail, had made a donation of £1,000 (£53,200 at today's values). This cheque was given on the personal recommendation of the Prince of Wales (later to become Edward VIII, before his abdication in 1936) and presented at St James's Palace. The Prince of Wales had visited clubs in Bermondsey in 1924 and had been impressed by the work of boys' clubs, as the 1927–28 annual report highlighted:

> *"On February 14, 1928, the Hon. Secretary of the Federation was received by HRH at St James's Palace, when the Prince expressed his high appreciation of the various boys' clubs in London, which he considered were doing work of the utmost value, and which provided more immediate results than many other forms of social service."*

Also in 1928, the BBC invited the Federation to make an appeal on behalf of clubs. The appeal, narrated by Wing Commander Louis Greig, raised £220. A new initiative to raise funds was the Dinner and Cabaret organised in the same year by Captain Buckmaster. The first occasion raised the sum of £300, which was invested in the Government of South Australia's 5% registered stock

The gift from Lord Rothermere was used to fulfil one of the Fed's long-standing aspirations-the purchase of its own playing field. The Fed had been dependent on the availability of the playing fields run by the LCC, though in 1912 and 1913 it had rented two grounds-one at Wormholt Farm and the other at Harrow Marshes in Lee-for football games. During the war, the number of playing fields had been depleted by their conversion to allotments and use for military purposes, and very few had been restored to their original use. Moreover, after the war, housing schemes had taken over many of the green fields which remained accessible from central London. The main pitches that remained in use post-war were those at Hackney Marshes, Parliament Hill Fields and Finsbury Park. But the arrangements for using even these pitches were far from satisfactory, as this Fed circular in 1919 revealed:

> *"It is an extraordinarily difficult matter ever to find a pitch, and, when you have found it, to erect the goalposts. It frequently happens that both goalposts at either end have to be held up during a match! Pitches seem to be numbered without any regular method, and in many cases either the referee or one of the teams has failed to find the ground."*

In February 1928, the Federation first discussed an offer from St Andrew's Home and Club to sell its ground in Northolt. The Federation also became aware that the Merchant Taylors' School ground at Bellingham and the ABS sports ground at Eden Park were available for purchase. It was finally decided to buy the Northolt grounds at a cost of £100 per acre for 15 acres of space. This was not the end of the quest for additional playing space: in May 1930, a newly constituted Grounds Sub-Committee agreed to a proposal that an application should be made to the London Parochial Charities for a grant of £5,000 for the purchase and development of playing fields, 'of which that at Northolt is the first'.

The year 1927 saw the launch of 'Mates', a new monthly journal at a price of one penny. In its first edition in February, it was quick to affirm the interdependent relationship between the Federation and its member clubs, both big and small:

> *"Our clubs are 'turnings', so to speak, and our Federation is the 'main street'...We want to remember that the 'main street' is as much the property of the little clubs as of the big clubs. We want to remember that we are all part of the show in our Federation. There's room for all in it, and the more we use this 'main street', the better shall we come to know and respect one another. 'Mates', that's it."*

The early issues of 'Mates' give a number of interesting cameos of long established clubs in membership of the Federation, and one article provides a snapshot of a typical 'Club Night':

> *"Let me take you on a fleeting visit to a Boys' Club. No matter which Fed club you pick, rich or poor, large or small, the happenings in any one are almost alike. The club opens at eight o'clock, but we arrive about half-past in order to let the boys gather.*
>
> *We first steal into what I should term the common room, as it is here the boys generally assemble. That window over there is where the boys book up for their games, and the gentleman on the other side is the Club Manager.*

Over yonder, you see the boys indulging in games of billiards, and the group leaning on the canteen counter are discussing whether to go running or to get some cricket practice instead."

One of the regular themes in 'Mates' in 1928 was the opportunity of emigration for young men who had little prospect of employment in the depressed economic conditions of the time. An advert in the March 1928 edition announced: 'Boys and Youth are wanted all the time for the farms of Canada'. Reduced passage rates were offered. On arrival, boys were placed with farmers at a recognised, guaranteed rate of pay, with board, lodging, washing and mending. After a few years' experience, 'a lad ought to be in a position to start on a farm of his own'. Applications had to be made to the Director of European Emigration for Canada, Canadian Building, Trafalgar Square, still the home of the Canadian Embassy today. Emigration was actively supported by the National Association of Boys' Clubs (NABC), which owned its own farm in Nova Scotia. The secretary of the national organisation wrote to the Fed at this time, conveying the message that the Hon. Secretary of the Colonisation Department would be pleased to visit any club to tell club boys of the opportunities secured for them through the NABC.

The editor appeared to encourage emigration with articles on 'What a chance for a boy' and 'A life in the open and a chance to be independent'. But the opportunities were not always so attractive to club members themselves. The February 1929 issue included a lively riposte from a club member, underlining that members did at times hold views and live lives that were at odds with those of their club managers, in an article entitled 'This Emigration Business: Why Lads Prefer England to Australia and Canada':

"In arranging these schemes, the emigration officials have entirely neglected to take into consideration the conditions under which the average club member exists, and their inevitable effect upon his outlook towards emigration, especially agricultural work.

The boy is usually one of a large family, living perhaps in a couple of rooms, at night sleeping in the same bed as one or two of his brothers, all huddling together in an endeavour to keep warm. Unlike the average public schoolboy, who rises through compulsion at an early hour, the young working lad keeps in bed until the last possible moment, the conditions at home producing in him a love of comfort and warmth. Consequently, when he hears of the 'wonderful open–air life' in Canada, it fails to move him. From the cinemas he has visited, he is led to believe that Canada's climate consists of snowstorms, blizzards and occasionally a flood or two to relieve the monotony– one cannot expect a town-bred youth to prefer this kind of life.

In London, he spends his leisure in clubs, cinemas, football matches, or dance halls (why club managers imagine that a dance hall is a den of vice and iniquity, I have yet to learn). If he emigrates, he is usually placed on a farm, miles from the nearest farm, so that within a few weeks of his arrival, he will be bored to death…

At the time of writing this article, I am out of work, and consequently 'sign on' three times a week. While attending the Labour Exchange one day, I heard a boy asked if he thought about emigrating. The reply was, 'Garn, wot d'you think I am–a herdsman of the wide open spaces?'"

The 1930s saw a new determination to take a more active role in promoting the welfare of working boys in the capital. A sub-committee was set up in July 1930 to consider the Federation's future development: the widening of its scope; its move to a new and larger headquarters; the financial implications of development and expansion; and a review of the constitution to enable the Fed to develop and expand.

In widening the scope of its work, the Federation affirmed its aim of providing adequate club premises, holiday facilities and playing fields 'for the physical, mental and social development of London working boys'. It sought to put in place a bureau of information on all matters relating to the boys' club movement and the general welfare of boys in London. It decided to pay more attention to the recruitment of new workers. National thinking also encouraged it to set its club-based work in the wider context of social welfare, reflecting the focus–spelled out in the NABC's 'Principles and Aims of the Boys' Movement' published in 1930–on fitness for citizenship, fitness for manhood and fitness for work. The NABC in 1931 published a handbook– 'A Guide to starting a boys' club and Hints on its management'–which argued that clubs had a broader role than merely keeping boys 'out of mischief':

> *"To play its part, and hold its own in the team of Boys' Organisations, a Boys' Club must not be considered a sort of vacuum cleaner to suck in boys off the streets, to collect them and leave them to their own devices, or to strain to entertain them by paltry forms of amusement. A Boys' Club must be directed by considered policy, and fulfil a definite purpose.*
>
> *A Club should train each of its members in character, see that he has a job which suits him, and promises a reasonable chance in life, that he takes up helpful forms of recreation, gets a proper holiday, and keeps in decent health."*

In the same year, a Federation report on 'Wider Aims and Finance' outlined the need to identify those areas of London in which clubs were urgently needed and to give financial help to new clubs. To help this process, a Survey and Statistical Sub–Committee was set up to research the number of school leavers and the spread of clubs in each Borough. To assist the future planning of boys' clubs, the Lord Mayor invited the Mayors of all London Boroughs to a meeting at the Mansion House.

Planned expansion on this scale demanded additional sources of income. Captain Buckmaster continued his successful dinner/cabarets. In 1930, Maurice Chevalier performed his songs, apparently his only performance on behalf of any charity in the country! A letter of appeal to livery companies, building on the links established at the 1927 Boxing Finals, produced 50 guineas from the Fishmongers' Company and £50 from the Clothworkers' Company.

By such means, the Federation managed to weather the storms of the depression years of the early 1930s. In the 1929–30 annual report, it had anticipated a 'testing' year:

> *"A number of large donations which had been received from public bodies and private individuals for several years have been withdrawn or reduced owing to financial stringency, and more than once during the year it has appeared probable that a serious deficit might have to be faced."*

But the Federation was protected from the economic problems by the continuing loyalty of its supporters. The number of Federates increased to 847, 97 over the previous year's figure. There was an increase in support by livery companies–the Armourers and Braziers, the Clothworkers, the Fishmongers, the Grocers, the Mercers and the Saddlers. The link with the NABC was also paying off, £92 being raised as the Federation's share of a joint appeal with the national organisation. The Federation was confident that its call on voluntary contributions could be justified by the importance of its work with boys, many of whom were unemployed:

> "In a time of general economic depression, when large sums have to be disbursed from rates and taxes to relieve distress and unemployment, it is natural to feel hesitation in pressing claims for voluntary contributions to social objectives, yet it is at such times, when so many young men have lost their occupation, that the boys' clubs of London are most needed to supply healthy recreation and interests, which are often alternative to vacant idling on the streets, or other less wholesome ways of employing an enforced leisure."

This commitment to offer boys and young men a lifeline at a difficult time prompted the Federation to redouble its efforts to set up a number of sub–committees to focus its activities– on the medical inspection of club members; on co–operation with the LCC in after–care work; on the proposed raising of the school leaving age; and on emigration. During this period, liaison between the Fed and the LCC had become so close that the Fed proposed to the LCC that its Education Department should nominate two representatives to serve on the Fed's sub– committee which dealt exclusively with the educational side of boys' clubs:

> "We have carefully considered the proposal, which, in effect, gives official recognition to what has been done in an unofficial way from time to time by officers of the Council. In the main, the educational needs of the boys can be met by facilities in or by the evening institutes, and we are of the opinion that any official co–operation will be to the benefit of the clubs and the institutes and obviate unnecessary overlapping."

Subsequently, the LCC Men's (Junior) Institutes became affiliated to the Federation, formalising the links between the two organisations and laying the foundations for a closer partnership between the statutory and voluntary sectors. This relationship gave club members access to a range of classes, such as carpentry, various hobbies, music and drama.

The Federation emerged from the crisis as a stronger organisation. Its membership had increased to 144 clubs with 12,000 boys in membership. In 1930, the Fed was able to realise its aspiration of giving grants to clubs, which would benefit from additional support: 24 clubs received grants of between £7 and £15. Both the Chairman and Hon. Secretary sat on the NABC governing body; the number of Federates had increased to 995, including nine Associates, four Fellows and three Companions. There was a proposal in 1930 that federates should play a role in visiting clubs, an anticipation of the subsequent importance that the Federation placed on membership development. Previously, Charles Wrench had seen the appointment of a paid secretary as a way of releasing him to make more visits of support to clubs, and a member of the executive committee had also taken on the role of visiting clubs seeking affiliation.

Waiting to be Weighed Boxing Competition 1931

The Federation's deepening sense of purpose led it to spell out its objectives in succinct form:

"1) To consolidate and extend the important work of boys' clubs in London

2) To promote competitions and friendly intercourse between members of affiliated clubs

3) To promote opportunities for those interested in the management of London working boys' clubs to interchange opinions as to the best way of conducting them."

The Federation also accelerated its efforts to influence social legislation. Many clubs had pioneered medical inspections: at the Hollington Club in Camberwell, for example, two doctors (Gallie and MacKenzie) introduced a system of medical inspection. (The Hollington Club had been taken over in 1921 by Dulwich College Mission, itself founded in 1886.) The Fed was keen to extend such schemes, since they afforded working boys continuing access to medical care:

> "The Committee desires to draw public attention to the fact that when boys leave school at 14 they are beyond the reach of school doctors, while they do not come within the scope of National Health Insurance until they are 16. It is regrettable also that for medical examinations in the LCC schools boys are not required to strip below the waist, so that cases of disease are not always discovered. Moreover, the strain on an immature lad's physique when he first enters industrial life may easily sew the seeds of future trouble, so that there is no period in a boy's life when his health needs more careful supervision. It is to be hoped that all club members will give this matter attention."

The Federation continued to press its view on these matters, and sent a deputation to the Board of Education, arguing strongly that all young persons between the ages of 14 and 16 should come within the provisions of the National Health Insurance scheme.

The Federation also lobbied to reduce the long hours of juvenile labour. It welcomed in 1932 the introduction of a new Children's Bill, but urged that it should be amended by the addition of clauses which put a limit on the hours that young people could work each day:

> "The great majority of people have no idea of the long hours worked by juveniles in unregulated industries. In practice, the Factory Acts limit the hours of labour of some boys, while large numbers are altogether unprotected. The Committee earnestly hopes that steps may be taken at the earliest possible date to prevent excessive hours of work for all juveniles."

The organisation was equally concerned about the impact of increasing unemployment on its members. At its annual conference in 1932, it discussed unemployment at some length, including an outline of the ways in which the Mary Ward Settlement gave help to the unemployed. At the 1933 conference, the focus was on the opportunities for boys in skilled and other trades:

> "Mr Wale–Smith pointed out that use of machinery had almost made the craftsman obsolete and that people employed in industry were now moreorless process workers. He detailed various organisations which seemed to offer favourable openings, and took the opportunity to warn those present of the difficulty of keeping pace with rapid changes in industry. A trade that today seems to offer good wages and favourable opportunities may, in a very few years, become overcrowded and ill–paid."

Additionally, the Federation sought to respond to the hardship and distress brought about by the economic decline in other parts of the country. 'The Link' (a successor to 'Mates') in its June 1934 edition attempted to convey the effect that the decline of ship–building had on the town of Jarrow:

"It is difficult for us here in London to imagine exactly what it means for 80% of the population of a town to be out of work for long periods. Perhaps the first thing that strikes one in going to such a town is the absence of traffic in the streets. There is no movement, no feeling of busyness. Shop after shop is boarded up and to let; even the pawnbrokers have gone out of business, for the people have nothing left to pawn. In the streets everyone moves slowly, as if trying to kill time. There is no reason to hurry when one has all day in which to do a thing. There are no distractions, no excitement; there is just nothing to do and, what is worse, nothing to look forward to."

The Fed decided to take practical action to give Jarrow boys at least something 'to look forward to', as the annual report of 1933–34 describes:

"A striking example during the year was the effort made by members of our affiliated clubs to ameliorate in some way the distressed conditions in Jarrow. Following the visit of a London club manager to this district, a talk was arranged at which the unfortunate plight of this town was made known to the meeting. Those present immediately expressed a desire to help, and a spontaneous collection was made. This ready response induced the Federation to acquaint all its clubs of the sad state of the Tyneside boys, and contributions were immediately forthcoming."

The fund quickly raised £81 (about £4,900 at today's values). 35 clubs responded to the appeal, which was allocated to the establishment of a boys' club in Jarrow.

At the Federation's annual conference in February 1935, Jimmy Mallon (the Warden of Toynbee Hall and a prominent social reformer) spoke on the raising of the school leaving age. The conference passed this resolution: "That this annual conference of London Boys' Club managers is of the opinion that for educational, industrial and social reasons the school leaving age should as soon as possible be raised to 15 years."

The Federation was clear and resolute in its antipathy and resistance to the rise of the Fascist movement, seeing its message as inimical to the values of the boys' club movement, as the editorial in the July 1934 edition of 'The Link' revealed:

"We hear much of youth movements in these days, and we see less happy countries where the generous and natural enthusiasm of the young are wrought, we would even say warped, for reasons of policy (may the Federation be permanently preserved from the Shirts).

It may be that we shall be called upon to answer the challenge of hard psychology and mass ideals. Our best answer would probably be to coin a half truth in the usual jargon and say, 'the team is the ideal mass movement of youth'. But, among ourselves, we might well elaborate a little and express more freely why we prefer the club to the cohort and the individual to the robot. Perhaps we should do it something after this fashion. We want to help boys to discover their creative faculties, to express themselves and to learn, by contacts in an ordered club, their obligations and their opportunities in an ordered society. We do not want to impose mass enthusiasms from without.

Boys will find their passionate loyalties. It is for us to help them in developing
the tendencies to proper thought and reflection, which will guide them to a right
judgement and in creating power to follow that judgement, come what may."

The conflict between the British Union of Fascists and the Jewish community in the East End
of London caused growing anger within the Federation. Its concern for the Jewish community,
and particularly for the large number of Jewish clubs in membership, prompted the Fed to write
this letter, which appeared in The Times on 5 November 1936:

"From time to time you have published letters dealing with the disorders in the
East End of London, and with the persistent and deplorable attempts to rouse
ill-feeling among sections of its population. Most of these letters deal very
naturally with wide considerations of politics and social organisation.

With politics as such, the LFBC has no concern whatsoever, but we number
among our members several Jewish clubs which, with their leaders, have made
no small contribution to the aims and ideals for which Boys' Clubs in this
country stand.

Holding, as we do, that mere fair-weather friendship is incompatible with the
spirit of co-operation and fellowship, which lies at the root of our organisation
in Britain, we desire to place on record, as publicly as we can, our real sympathy
with our Jewish members in the campaign of calumny and violence which has
been launched against them."

The letter elicited this gesture of solidarity from the Durham County Association of Boys' Clubs
to Basil Henriques of the Oxford and St George's Club:

"We have read the letter in The Times and are reminded that three years ago the
boy members of your settlement showed their sympathy for the boys of Jarrow
by sending money to help with the starting of a Boys' Club.

We wish now to send to you and your boys, on behalf of the County Association,
our very deep sympathy in the difficulties to which the letter refers, and our
indignation at the insults to which our Jewish fellow citizens are being exposed."

A major development in the 1930s was the acquisition of a lease of a playing field at Bellingham
in South London. It was purchased in 1933 from the Merchant Taylors' School by the City
Parochial Fund and leased to the Federation. The school authorities, however, took away all
the machines, rollers and other grounds maintenance equipment. This would have presented
an insuperable financial burden to the Fed, were it not for the generosity of the Carnegie Trust
and the National Playing Fields Association. Their financial help also enabled two hard tennis
courts and a new iron railing around the ground to be installed. Within the year, the Federation
had sold its ground at Northolt to the Inns of Court Mission, since it did not have the funds
available for its development.

Another change in these years was the replacement of the in-house journal, 'Mates', by 'The
Link'. 'Mates' had become too expensive to run, so 'The Link' was introduced on a smaller,

more cost–effective scale. It was still intended to fulfil the function of keeping the Fed, Federates and clubs in touch with each other. 'The Link' continued the tradition of 'Mates' in being critical of the approach of some club managers and in giving glimpses of the perspective of club members themselves, not usually given much space in the annual reports. The September 1929 edition of 'Mates' contained an article on 'Our Manager' by a club member:

> *"If there is any quality a manager should possess, it is the art of understanding the boy. I, myself, feel that club managers are too prone to 'preach' to the members, and I know that boys are not quite over in love with being urged to play the game, not to swear and gamble. The boy is quite aware it is wrong to do these things–he learnt it ages ago, and it is not the duty of managers to carry on the work of the boys' former school masters, and not act as if members had no conception of what the term 'Public School Spirit' means. After all, the public school boys were never taught good sportsmanship as a subject."*

This rather more sceptical perspective was reinforced in the September 1933 issue of 'The Link', when a Mr Yorkshire was critical of the older generation of club leaders:

> *"He is definitely suggesting that many of them are inclined to become somewhat cranky, that they should study the ordinary common–or–garden British boy as though he were some extraordinary specimen of the jungle. They watch his habits minutely, they analyse his motions, study his actions and reactions, delve into his psychology, divide him up into physical, mental and spiritual spheres, and so on."*

Some familiar themes recurred in the early 1930s. A deficit of £294 was recorded in 1931–32, compared with the previous year's £126 surplus. The annual report accepted that this deterioration reflected the prevailing economic climate: 'taking into consideration the extreme financial stringency throughout the country, this falling off is not altogether surprising'. The demand for the Fed's services showed no sign of abating, however. By 1932–33, the number of clubs had increased to 172 (127 in 1931–32), with a total membership of 11,500 boys (9,500 in 1931–32). This increase was explained to some extent by the affiliation of 16 Post Office Institutes. (Two additional organisations, with similar aims and objectives to the Federation, affiliated their member clubs in 1935–36–the London Diocesan Boys' Union and the Catholic Youth Federation.) In many ways, this expansion was the result of the Federation's concern to extend its scope and influence. In 1934–35, a Development Sub–Committee was set up, with its own full–time Secretary (H.L.Hollis of the Westminster School Mission), whose salary was guaranteed by John Scott, a member of the committee. This was the first instance of a focused and dedicated commitment on the part of the Fed to the developmental function, supported by a designated member of staff. Though the main thrust of the new sub–committee was to give advice and assistance to new clubs starting up, the Development Secretary was given the task of visiting clubs, so that the Fed could keep in closer touch with clubs and put them in touch with each other–a task which became a distinctive and central part of the Fed's servicing of clubs over the following decades. In the 1935–36 annual report, the Federation was able to claim a membership of 200 clubs and 15,000 boys. This growth led to the establishment of a Finance Committee for the first time, which faced a 'formidable' deficit of £263 (approximately

£15,730 at today's values). This was attributable not to increasing expenditure or diminishing subscriptions, but to an absence in the year of any special fundraising initiatives. The lack of activity on this front prompted the Federation to make a special appeal in 1937, its Golden Jubilee Year, to all subscribers to obtain at least one other subscriber during the year. The appeal made £2,041, of which £1,000 was allocated to the Grant–in–Aid fund (to be awarded to individual clubs for particular purposes). Other donors were Clement Attlee (then the Leader of the Labour Party), his wife and the Duke of Windsor (the title of Edward VIII after his abdication), who donated £250.

The 50th anniversary of the organisation saw the Federation look back with some astonishment and pride on its development and growth since its inception in 1887:

> *"In those early days, the Federation was sadly handicapped by lack of man–power, money and public interest, but the early pioneers were convinced of the worthiness of the cause, and struggled through inconceivably difficult times with always the confident hope that one day their foundling would occupy a commanding place on the public's list of deserving causes."*

But the sense of pride was accompanied by a steely determination to face any new challenges the future might hold:

> *"Now, in 1937, the Committee looks back at those years of struggle, with relief that they are over, but with the knowledge that almost certainly the future has in store many difficulties and trials, perhaps more complex than those which faced its predecessors. Still, it has the comforting reflection that this great movement, started so humbly in 1887, has become a necessary and important part of the social structure of London."*

Certainly, the public profile of the Federation was at this time a more visible one: the Evening Standard initiated a regular column which presented news of club activities and developments; the Evening News carried a series of articles written by one of its journalists who visited several clubs.

Even the financial situation, a constant source of worry, was eased by the increase of the grant from the City Parochial Charities to £1,500. This sum was allocated to the Fed's current priorities–£250 for developmental purposes and £1,000 as grants to affiliated clubs (the remaining £250 went towards the upkeep of the Bellingham sports ground, which was proving to be costly to run). The Grant–in–Aid fund enabled the Federation to deliver its long–held aspiration that it should be in a position to help individual clubs, particularly in those cases where an injection of money would make a crucial difference between survival and extinction. In 1937, a City banquet, held at the Hall of the Worshipful Company of Grocers, made a profit of £2,000, half of which was allocated to the Grant–in–Aid scheme. One of the speakers at the banquet was Clement Attlee. In 1938, the Federation's Patron, Prince Arthur of Connaught, died. The tribute in the annual report traced his influence since he assumed the role in 1904:

"He had watched (the Federation) grow from a small and obscure organisation into the prominent position it occupies in the life of London today. His HRH was always heavily interested in the welfare of the Fed, and ready to help the cause of boys' clubs in whatever way lay in his power."

In the 1936–37 annual report, the Federation had expressed its concern that, though the aims of its clubs were widely understood, it had not sufficiently realised the help it could obtain from other bodies, especially the LCC. Closer links began to develop with the introduction of the Physical Training Recreation Act of 1937. This legislation gave clubs access to a fund set up by the Government to enlarge or improve their accommodation. Increasing co–operation with the LCC's Education Department also meant that instructors were provided for classes held in clubs 'in almost any subject for which a sufficient number of boys show a willingness to enrol'.

The growth in the Federation's activities led to an expansion in its complement of full–time staff: an Assistant Secretary and an Assistant Development Officer were appointed, bringing the number of full–time staff to four. Another indication of increased activity was the purchase by the London Parochial Charities of Essex County Cricket Club's ground at Leyton, for the joint use of the Fed and the London Union of Girls' Clubs (the pavilion is still the home of Leyton Youth Centre).

Handicrafts Class, 1938

3. The Era of Solidarity, 1939–1959

Developments during the Second World War marked something of a watershed in the growth of the Youth Service. War–time conditions created a new sense of solidarity and social cohesion, which diminished some of the more acute pre–war social differences built around wealth, status and function. The experience of neighbourliness at a local level led A.J.P.Taylor to describe the war years as a 'brief period when the English people felt that they were a fully democratic community'.

In the early years of the war, however, the dislocation and confusion prompted an apprehension that there could be a serious outbreak of public disorder. Circular 1486, called 'The Service of Youth' and issued in November 1939 by the Board of Education, had no hesitation in pinpointing the social problems which afflicted young people and could harm the social cohesiveness of the country:

> *"Today the black–out, the strain of war and the disorganisation of family life*
> *have created conditions, which constitute a social menace to youth."*

The evacuation of children from urban areas to rural settings initially heightened the sense of acute social differences, and the blitz created a stark fear among the authorities that uncontrollable incidents would occur if the population were assembled in large public shelters.

As the nation began to experience a sense of solidarity as it contended with the threat of invasion, it learned to overcome the horror of a potentially anti–social youth and to develop a more positive sense of the capacities of young people and the contribution they could make to the war effort. The need to create a new social cohesion in responding to the conditions of war meant that young people were unreservedly accepted as partners in combating a shared adversity. All the circulars which were released during the war years to give direction to the Youth Service stressed the role of young people as partners in a common enterprise, arguing that direct expression should as a matter of course be given to the views of young people and that they should be encouraged to play an informed and responsible part in society. The report of the Youth Advisory Council appointed by the Board of Education in 1942 sums up the mood of the times in its acknowledgement of the right of young people to reach their own views and contribute as citizens to society as a whole:

> *"…the kind of society we wish to see, that is, a society which can only function*
> *effectively if all its members take an informed and responsible share in its*
> *activities…We neither expect nor wish all young people to grow up holding the*
> *same views, for if they did both they and the body politic would be the poorer."*

Circular 1486 represented an important step forward in the recognition of youth work as a national initiative and service. The Board of Education took on direct responsibility for youth welfare. The circular also recommended the creation of local Youth Committees, based on co-operation between local education authorities and voluntary organisations, which would have an important brief of determining local needs and formulating coherent policies. Funds were made available to support clubs in appointing leaders, in hiring premises and in purchasing equipment. Circular 1516, 'The Challenge to Youth', published in 1940, was an attempt to offer guidance on 'the general aim and purpose of the work' which the Youth Committees had been set up to supervise. The circular was adamant that the overriding purpose of the 'social and physical training' which it saw as central to the work of the new national service was 'to fit young people for membership of a free society'. In seeking a harmonious balance between voluntary effort and statutory support, the circular defined the function of the State in these terms:

"...to focus and lead the efforts of all engaged in youth welfare; to supplement the resources of existing national organisations without impairing their independence; and to ensure through co–operation that the ground is covered in a way never so far attained."

Circular 1543 on 'Youth Service Corps', issued by the Board of Education in 1941, asserted that one of the chief attractions of the Corps to young people was that it enabled them to 'acquire a recognised status in the community' and 'to learn and practise lessons of initiative, self–giving and self–government'.

This was the challenging context in which the Federation had once again to prove its resilience and capacity to survive in adverse circumstances. In a speech at the first Boys' Conference held at Nazeing in May 1939, W.McG. Eagar contrasted the boys' club movement's belief in the value of each individual to the treatment of individuals as 'atoms' in a totalitarian state. 'The Link' published his summary of the speech:

"I emphasised that the adult club leaders who were present were not there to tell the boys what they thought or ought to think, but merely to help them think and express their thoughts. I suggested that democracies are now on their trial at the bar of history, and can only survive and justify themselves as forms of society if they allow their members to think freely, vigorously and constructively. There are many countries which only 10 or 15 years ago had youth movements which were like our own in being voluntary movements, carried on in an atmosphere of kindliness and designed to enable their members to grow up into strong and healthy men, of different types, according to the views they wished to adopt and the religions to which they belonged. Now membership of those youth movements was compulsory and all their members had to conform precisely to the ideas of the political party in power. We have to ask ourselves whether our own idea of the State, which to its adult citizens is very much what the club is to its members, is the right form of State for us; whether it worked; how it could be put right if it was not working well; and who was to put it right. At the present time, unfortunately, we had to be clear in our own minds whether our idea of a State was worth defending, and how and by whom it was to be defended."

The fear that the war would cause an immediate closure of clubs was not realised. The Fed News (a change of name from 'The Link') of December 1939 commented that the blackout had not been helpful to the continued running of clubs, 'but people are gradually getting used even to this, and are developing cats' eyes'.

The absence of Federation's records and annual reports from 1938 to 1950 makes it difficult to gain a full impression of the organisation's development during the Second World War, but the gap can be filled and a picture assembled to some extent by the surviving records of a number of affiliated clubs. The different stages of the war, and their impact on the clubs' programme, can be gauged from the annual reports of the Crown and Manor Boys' Club in Hoxton (the club was the result of a merger between the Crown Club, founded in 1926 in association with Winchester College, the public school, and the Hoxton Manor Club, established in 1920, itself a successor of the Claude Eliott Lads' Club founded in 1906). In its annual report of 1939–40, it illustrated how London in September 1940 had withstood three weeks of continuous night bombardments:

> "At the Club attendance has naturally fallen, but we have twenty or thirty boys regularly every night. We have, of course, had to adapt the Club programme temporarily to the new situation. We hope to continue with weekend activities such as football. But in the evenings we now open at 5.30 pm, and members come as early as they can to get through some training in the gym before the sirens or perhaps to have a run through the streets while daylight lasts. The hot showers now fulfil a greater need than ever. Then when the guns open up we adjourn to the newly built shelter and carry on. The shelter, an excellent strong one, consists of two fair-sized rooms, one of which is reserved for 'quiet activities' such as table games and letter writing to Old Boys. We have also seized the opportunity to re-direct our energies to forms of activity more directly concerned with grim reality, such as classes in First Aid and the control of incendiary bombs."

The 1940–41 annual report stated that, as the second year of the war drew to its close, 'it is a matter of gratitude that the Club survives with undiminished activity'. In sustaining these activities, the report praised the 'unfailing and unflagging' help and encouragement of the Federation. Yet the continuing survival of the club did mean that it had to gear its 'undiminished' activity to very exceptional circumstances, as this advice to boys included in the September edition of the club magazine demonstrates:

> "Here are some things to bear in mind.
>
> 1. Tell your family about the Club's shelter and always let them know when you are going to the Club, so that they need not be anxious about you.
>
> 2. Find out if they would like you to come home as soon as possible when the warning goes or if they prefer you to stay at the Club. For the time being, it is unlikely that any boy will be allowed to leave the Club once the warning has sounded.
>
> 3. Always carry your gas-mask to and fro with you. We are warned that this is a wise precaution and it is simply silly to ignore it.
>
> 4. Think out all the useful activities which might be carried out in the shelter and suggest them. There are two compartments to the shelter. One can be for games: the other for quiet activities
>
> Here are one or two suggestions of ours:

(a) Letter–writing. You can write letters to the Old Boys just as well in the shelter as anywhere–rather better, in fact, as you are not missing any training thereby.

(b) First Aid. Join the Tuesday evening class. We want at least twenty regular attendees. Last Tuesday there were only sixteen.

(c) Course in how to deal with Incendiary Bombs, and other ARP classes. We hope to start these right away.

5. Please do what you are asked to do promptly. Don't always argue or expect reasonable explanations on the nail. After all, this is an unreasonable world.

6. If you or your family have suffered as a result of air raids, or if you know of any Club boy who has suffered, please let us know at once. We want to help as much as we can, but it is very likely we shall not get to know in time unless everyone cooperates. But only tell us what you KNOW. Don't spin yarns."

The 1941–42 annual report depicted the year as one of consolidation after the disruption of the blitz:

"Freedom from raids has enabled us in the Club to consolidate and develop a programme balanced between pre–Service training and those normal activities which have good citizenship as their aim."

The regularity, if not the normality, of this routine is the theme of the 1942–43 annual report:

"The fourth year of the war and the Club's life has passed very quickly; the reason is that since the London blitz stopped we have been able to return to a regular routine. Regular but not normal: hardly (any club) leads a life that in 1939 would have been called normal. Longer hours of work (fortunately and recently reduced by HM Government to a maximum of 44 hours for boys under 16) and higher wages war against the spirit of club life, while the prospect of medicals at 17 and three–quarters and calling up for the Services produces a state of unrest in the working boy's mind which probably has its parallel in secondary school as well."

In the 1945–46 report, the club welcomed the completed first year of its life free 'from the alarms of war with Germany'. Its membership quickly reached 150, with a waiting list for the first time since the pre–war years.

It would seem that the pattern of club life traced in the Crown and Manor records was a familiar one across London. Club activities were generally affected by the departure of senior members and Old Boys who were called up to serve in the Armed Forces. For example, by September 1940, the number of Crown and Manor Old Boys in HM Forces totalled 104. In 1941, it was reported that, as a result of this scale of loss, the number of London boys' clubs had been seriously reduced. Another cause of this reduction was the destruction of some clubs buildings in air raids. The oldest club, St Andrew's, was directly affected when its premises were destroyed by an enemy bomb on 11 November 1940. Temporary accommodation was provided by Westminster City Council, and fund–raising for a new club began (a new club was eventually opened on the site of the old building in 1958).

The war conditions also affected the programme of clubs. Football games and competitions were limited by the shortage of pitches in LCC parks. Handicrafts were curtailed by the difficulty in obtaining materials. But, despite all these obstacles, the Federation succeeded in organising London-wide competitions in boxing, cross-country, swimming, drama, essay writing and general knowledge. First Aid classes were supplemented by 'anti-gas' and other Air Raid Precautions (ARP) classes. In many clubs, a rota of boys acted as 'spotters' during air raids, detecting and reporting fires. Members formed themselves into auxiliary rescue parties, when buildings and houses were damaged by bombs. Micky Davies, the leader of the Vallance Boys' Club in Spitalfields, organised his members into fire-parties, which involved the boys in rescue work and help to the victims of air raids–rescuing people from collapsing buildings, putting out innumerable fires with their own fire-fighting equipment and looking after the wounded. The boys of Alford House formed an army cadet company and kept vigilant guard to preserve the club buildings from fire damage.

The economies of war did cause the Fed News to be suspended. This was precipitated by the paper shortage, but it was also considered something of a luxury to produce a magazine at a time of economic restraint (these considerations may also explain the absence of Federation annual reports during this time).

As well as maintaining as full a programme of activities as possible during the war, as it had done during the First World War, the Federation sought to develop new initiatives in response to the prevailing conditions. In 1938, it launched a City Lunch Club, which continued throughout the war. Though most factories provided canteens and recreational facilities, no particular provision was made for young people who worked in services connected to the City of London. The club, open to boys between the ages of 14 and 19, was first located in Love Lane, but its premises were destroyed by a bomb in December 1940. The Grocers' Company offered alternative accommodation in the Grocers' Hall in Princess Street. The lunch club provided 'a hot, wholesome meal' at a cost of only fifteen pence, and opportunities for indoor recreation, like table tennis, chess and draughts, were also made available. Membership grew to over a hundred boys, and an average of 80 boys lunched there every day. A British Council article on the club reported:

> "Physical and Mental Fitness are principles which are attracting a great deal of attention these days, particularly where the welfare of youth is concerned...(The boys) find at the club a place where they can not only get a really good lunch, but also mingle freely with their contemporaries, and exchange news and views."

Interestingly, as an indication of the war-time conditions, even a photograph illustrating this article has a note that it was 'passed by the censor'! The rifle range built in the roof of the Crown and Manor Boys' Club is another reminder that the country was on a war footing, though the club integrated the activity into its curriculum by asserting that 'rifle shooting is excellent training for hand, eye and muscle'.

Instruction at the Club's Miniature Rifle Shooting Range

The Federation also continued to offer training courses throughout the war. In some Boroughs, senior boys were invited to join the Borough Youth Committee's advisory council, so that they could inform the committee of the attitudes of young people to current issues. A number of clubs forged close links with Labour Exchanges, making every effort to persuade boys to leave 'dead end' jobs and take up a trade.

The Federation remained in a strong position after the Second World War to plan for the future in a systematic and realistic way. The 1944 Education Act had strengthened the role of the State and local education authorities in making it the duty of every local education authority 'to secure facilities for further education, including adequate facilities for recreation and social and physical training'. But the Act was at pains to insist that local education authorities should have regard for the 'expediency' of co-operating with voluntary bodies. In its response to this new relationship, the Fed was fully aware that social changes might necessitate new responses:

> *"The fluctuations in the birth rate, the movement of population from one area to another and the changing educational and moral standards of young people were factors which must influence the future pattern of boys' clubs in our capital city. Vague generalisations must give way to hard facts and action must follow discussion."*

The 'hard facts' were these: a sharp rise in the birth rate meant that the number of boys of club age would steadily increase until 1965; the traditional centres for club work, such as Bermondsey and Stepney, were no longer teeming with young people; the number of young people receiving some form of continued education beyond the age of 15 had increased considerably since 1939, and–with money to spend on recreation–they had different expectations of what clubs should offer in terms of activities.

After the war, the Federation pushed on in new directions to meet the changing needs. It initiated a Development section to support and guide the foundation of new clubs, to replace those which had been damaged or destroyed in the war and to improve old clubs. Woodrow High House in Amersham, Buckinghamshire was donated to the Federation in 1945 by the Worshipful Company of Goldsmiths (the company had bought the Seventeenth Century manor house–once home to the family of Oliver Cromwell–from Sir Nigel Leslie, High Sheriff of Buckinghamshire in 1937). Its acquisition enabled the Federation to increase the training of managers and boys. The grant that the LCC's Higher Education Sub-Committee made to the training centre in the 1946–47 financial year was the first time that it had given grant-aid to a training establishment. Its minutes of 10 December 1946 record its deliberations which led to this decision:

> *"LFBC proposes to utilise Woodrow High House, Amersham for a training centre for paid and voluntary club leaders and senior members of boys' clubs in the Federation's area.*
>
> *The training of full–time youth leaders will be in the nature of refresher courses of 1–2 weeks' duration or over a series of weekends for voluntary workers for similar periods and will deal with general club technique and specialised activities. There will also be introductory or assessment courses for men and women contemplating entry into youth work and short courses in general sociology and 'neighbourhood interest'. The training of senior boys will be designed to equip them to undertake more responsible activities in their clubs and to awaken their interest in local government, politics and the arts, and to assist them to follow up these subjects at university extension lectures.*
>
> *The Council has not so far aided an establishment of this kind, although it has given a small number of bursaries to assist club leaders to attend short courses arranged by the National Voluntary Youth Organisations.*
>
> *Having regard to the fact that about two–thirds of clubs affiliated to the Federation are within the Administrative County of London, we are of the opinion that, as an experiment, a grant not exceeding £600 could be justified for the year ending 30 September 1947, subject to the Federation forwarding a full report on its activities at Woodrow High House and a statement of accounts for the period as soon after its expiry as possible."*

This grant of £600 was to be used in aid of the maintenance of the premises. The Federation also received a grant of £1,000 from the Ministry of Education.

The value of the training courses at Woodrow High House is recognised in this extract from the Crown and Manor's annual report of 1947–48:

"A Senior Boys' course normally covers two weekends, and in spite of the limited time its effects are astonishing. Boys are taken right out of their normal surroundings, thrown together with unknown boys from the clubs, and given, it seems, an entirely new outlook on life in human society."

Woodrow also held at this time, in a spirit of post–war reconciliation, an International Fortnight, in which 12 London boys met up with 8 boys from the British Zone of Germany and smaller contingents from France and Holland.

Woodrow High House, The Federation Training Centre Near Amersham

In 1947, the Federation marked its Diamond Jubilee with a full schedule of celebrations and events, including a Thanksgiving Service at St Paul's Cathedral; a garden party at Woodrow High House; a performance of J.M.Barrie's 'The Boy David', at the Scala Theatre in the presence of Princess Margaret; and a banquet at Goldsmith's Hall, when the principal guest was Field Marshall Montgomery.

This was also the year in which HRH The Prince Philip Duke of Edinburgh became Patron of the Federation, the very first charity of which he assumed that role. He quickly embarked on a series of visits to clubs, which have been a hallmark of his continuing involvement with the organisation. (By the end of 2012, he had fulfilled 117 engagements.) His first round of visits in December 1948 involved nine clubs –Aldenham, Alford House, Brunswick, Oxford and Bermondsey, Crown and Manor, North West Jewish, PM, St Joseph's Rotherhithe and Thornton. The Crown and Manor's annual report described his visit there:

> *"On the 3rd December, the Club was honoured by a visit from the Patron of the LFBC, HRH the Duke of Edinburgh, with Ian Leslie in attendance. The ordinary Wednesday evening activities were in progress; the secret of the Duke's visit had been so well kept that only a few minutes before his arrival a few boys began to drift home after P.T., and had to be recalled. His Royal Highness was shown around the Club by three of the boys–George Thecker, Tony Blower and Charlie Compton–and he spent more than an hour finding out all about us."*

Charlie Compton, one of the boys to show the Duke of Edinburgh around the club, went on to become a full–time youth worker at the club, a path which was to be followed by many members of Fed clubs in the post–war years as the Youth Service created more opportunities of this kind.

In 1948, the Federation took part in a new form of fund raising, Club Week, which was to be an effective and dependable source of income over the next few decades. The aim of the scheme, in response to the financial duress of the times, was to raise the profile of the boys' club movement (at local, regional and national level) and to build up finances on a broader and firmer basis by appealing to a much larger public. Club members themselves raised funds through the sale of raffle tickets and other efforts, and the income was shared between the individual club, the Federation and the NABC.

Clubs also received for the first time direct funding from the LCC towards the salaries of club leaders. In October 1938, the LCC had assumed the responsibility for youth work from the Joint Council of London Juvenile Organisations Committee. The London Youth Committee came into being in February 1940, establishing youth committees in each Metropolitan Borough and making small emergency grants to youth units towards the cost of equipment and minor building adaptations. The 1944 Education Act established the principle that clubs should be eligible for grant-aid for salaries, and the first grants were awarded in 1947. The Crown and Manor Boys' Club in that year received £150 (about £4,970 at today's values) towards the £380 cost (£12,590 now) of its manager's salary and pension contribution. (By 1955–56, this grant had been increased to £325.) The club's manager and club leader at this time was Jimmy Doyle. He had been a member of the club, worked as a handyman and assistant leader and went on to become manager in 1941. He had previously been employed as manager of the Campion Club in Pitfield Street, where the offices of London Youth are now based.

The formation of the Welfare State also influenced the range of services that some clubs came to provide. Alford House (which had been helped by a Ministry of Education grant under the Social and Physical Training Grants Regulations to move from its former premises in Lambeth

Walk to renovated premises in Aveline Street) accommodated one of the LCC's maternity and child welfare centres and two old people's clubs as well as its traditional youth provision.

The 1950–51 annual report posed three urgent questions for the Federation to address in the changing post–war context:

"can existing clubs absorb a larger membership to meet the increased birth rate of the 1940s?

are these clubs situated in the right places?

do present club activities take into account the improved standards of education, and do they still cater for a boy's desire to experiment and to find new interests and outlets for self–expression?"

The Federation was organisationally well positioned to meet these new challenges. In 1950, its complement of full–time staff had increased to seven: a General Secretary (David Cornock–Taylor), an Assistant Secretary, five Development Officers, and a Boys' Club Shop Manager. It had access to two sports grounds–Bellingham and an additional acquisition in the form of the Eltham ground in Avery Hill (often referred to in the Federation's records as the Sydney Franklin Playing Field because of his donation to its acquisition; Franklin was later to become a donor and supporter of the Samuel Montagu Boys' Club, in close proximity to the ground).

The number of clubs had, however, been declining. Some charitable bodies and private donors were withdrawing their support, in the belief that more public money was now available for youth work undertaken by voluntary organisations–a belief that the Fed was quick to describe as 'mistaken'. These developments put more onus on the Development Officers to nurture local initiatives, to plan projects to fill the gaps left by the diminution in spontaneous voluntary action and to argue the case for clubs to be more adventurous in retaining the support of the boys 'beset with influences which distract them and may even bewilder them'. It was not easy for clubs to survive in these conditions, as the history of the Addison Boys' Club in Hammersmith typifies. A club had operated in the area since 1937, but had been forced to close due to lack of funding in 1950. The club was reopened in 1953 as the Addison Boys' Club, underpinned by grants from the Ministry of Education, the London Federation, the NABC and Hammersmith Youth Committee. (In the 1970s, a deteriorating building and difficulties in finding suitable leadership caused the club once again to fold. It recommenced operations in 1978, facilitated by grants from the Department of Education and Science, the London Federation, the NABC and the Variety Club.)

This changing context persuaded the Federation that it should direct its intervention to three main ends. to give maximum help to existing clubs in areas where the future need would be the greatest; to encourage the transfer from 'overclubbed' to 'underclubbed' boroughs of certain well–founded clubs; and to concentrate the development of new clubs in those same areas.

There were signs in the post-war period that the Fed's sources of funding were changing. The LCC was allocating additional public funds to the organisation–both by grants to the clubs, sports grounds and the training centre and by means of a generous donation from its Sunday Cinematograph Fund.

Nevertheless, the financial situation was depicted as precarious, particularly when the NABC was forced, due to its own financial difficulties, to discontinue for a time its grant to the Fed (which, in the 1950–51 financial year, amounted to £5,000, approximately the equivalent of £145,000 today). The Federation continued, therefore, to face the perennial challenge of identifying new sources of income. It appealed to clubs to support the Fed's activities, especially the Boxing Finals at the Royal Albert Hall, to purchase sports and games equipment and clothing from the Boys' Club Shop (the new name of the Co–operative Sports Supply Association) and to help raise income from subscriptions and donations to at least £4,500. Despite these continuing financial pressures, the Fed was able to make grants of £3,440 to 77 clubs, supported by donations from the Goldsmiths' Company, the Port of London Authority and the Guinness Company Trust Fund.

The appeal was successful enough for the Federation to report in the 1951–52 annual report that income from subs and donations had increased from £2,694 in 1948–49 to £4,419 in 1951–52, very close to its appeal target. The main contributions in the form of grants came from the LCC (£1,545) and the London Parochial Charities (£700). Income was boosted further by three special fundraising events: an art exhibition in Old Bond Street; a dinner organised by the Worshipful Company of Fishmongers at its hall; and a world film premiere of 'Ivanhoe' at the Empire Theatre, Leicester Square organised by the Variety Club of Great Britain. Club Week in 1951 raised £2,500. A Director of Appeals was appointed for the first time in 1952, with the clear intention of implementing a policy of financial independence and relieving the administrative staff of fundraising activities.

The role of the Development Officers was becoming more influential, and this title was changed to Field Officer, perhaps indicating the extent of their involvement in supporting clubs at the grass roots. They played a crucial role in developing clubs for the under–14s, a widening of the Fed's remit to work with boys still at school. 60 clubs, with a membership of 3,000 boys, quickly became affiliated, all run by voluntary club leaders and committees. A further 2,000 boys of this age group, it was estimated, were members of clubs which did not provide a separate section.

The Field Officers also assumed responsibility for training, as the Federation sought to organise its training programme on a more structured basis. A conference in the spring of 1952 was typical of the new rigour which they brought to the training of voluntary leaders and helpers: it gave advice and help on a wide range of practical problems; it outlined youth work methods; and it included a visit to a neighbouring club as an illustration of effective approaches. The availability of Woodrow High House as a training centre helped to give new impetus to the training programme. A full and varied schedule of courses was held throughout the year at the centre, on such subjects as instruction in arts and crafts activities, 'helping the club work' and self–government.

The Federation was able to state, in its annual report for 1952–53, that the number of clubs had increased from 260 to 271, a high point in membership levels in these decades. It commented that this slight increase defied the current trend of decline experienced by the majority of youth organisations. Part of the problem of sustaining clubs in this period was the difficulty of attracting experienced and enthusiastic adults to join club management committees. But it was clear that the Federation could not look to the traditional sources of support that had been the hallmark of its development in its earlier years:

"In those early days, Bermondsey and other London Boroughs were full of Oxford and Cambridge men sharing their interests and indeed their lives with members of Boys' Clubs. How much has changed in 50 years! Gone are those days of hunger, insecurity, overcrowding and unemployment, and gone are also many of the men from Oxford and Cambridge. Only a handful remain to carry on the traditions of the past and to give the leadership, religious inspiration and love which are needed as much today as ever."

The Fed continued to attempt to attract more men from universities, but had increasingly to accept that 'the approaches have not been heralded by the sound of trumpet calls'. In any case, the nature of youth work was changing, and the Federation's clubs benefited from the services of full-time professional youth workers. It was disappointed, however, by the rapid turnover of the leaders, by the inadequacy of their remuneration and lack of prospects. A deputation was organised to meet the Chief Executive of the LCC on this matter, submitting a proposed salary scale for youth workers. The response of the London Youth Committee (LYC) within the LCC's committee structure in June 1952 was less than wholehearted:

"The London Youth Committee agrees that the value of adequate scales of remuneration in attracting and retaining suitable leaders should not be underestimated, but they point out that the Youth Service is essentially a vocation and harm may result if salary is made a matter of supreme importance. We should mention here that our grants section in their dealings with individual youth units applying to the Council for grant encourages the payment of adequate salaries to qualified leaders employed by voluntary organisations."

The LYC did, however, agree to enter into discussions with London voluntary youth organisations and the University of London Institute of Education about the training of youth leaders. Low levels of remuneration remained an issue, nonetheless. In 1957, a further discussion revealed that, of 109 full-time paid leaders of youth groups seeking financial aid from the LCC, 81 received less than £510 per annum, which was the minimum of the scale adopted for qualified leaders by the Federation.

Despite the introduction of the Welfare State and the professionalisation of the Youth Service, the Federation still had to maintain its work in challenging social conditions:

"In spite of the great strides which have been made in the last century in health and education, it is a disagreeable fact that 17% of the recruits enlisting for national service are rejected on medical grounds and 6.6% of recruits are found to be illiterate or semi-literate.

Perhaps more than ever before the voluntary youth organisations of our
country have a challenge to face. It has been established beyond doubt that the
Welfare State cannot cater for each and every individual problem, and clearly
in this land at present there are many unfit boys who ought to be fit, and many
illiterate boys who ought to be able to read and write."

Yet, to face this challenge, the Fed needed to attract increased funding. In the 1953–54 annual report, its position was described as 'perilous' and in 1954–55 as 'grave'. The continuing problem was that the survival of the organisation depended on regular income to cover its yearly expenditure and additional funds to build up adequate resources for future development. The Fed was able to budget for its annual income of £16,000 (about £300,000 at today's prices): the main sources of income were subs/donations (£4,441), the profits from the Boys' Club Shop (£1,513), and grants from the NABC (£1,500), the Sunday Cinematograph Fund (£1,083) and the London Parochial Charities (£400). Additionally, the London Federation of Working Men's Clubs, on its dissolution, donated its assets to the Federation to support its work among its Old Boys' Clubs. But this income did not allow the Federation to plan for the future. So, in 1955, a new initiative– 'Sponsor a Boy'–was launched. Its objective was to provide funds for additional clubs and the Federation, and to encourage more people to take a personal interest in boys' clubs. London was divided into six areas under the patronage of sportsmen elected by the boys of the clubs in those areas. The sportsmen were three athletes (Roger Bannister, Chris Chataway and Gordon Pirie), a footballer (Stanley Matthews), a cricketer (Frank Tyson) and a boxer (Dai Dower). In addition to traditional donors like the livery companies and charitable trusts, the scheme attracted the support of businesses, such as HSBC, ICI, Hoover, Watney and Cornhill Insurance.

In May 1956, David Cornock–Taylor resigned after seven years as General Secretary. The annual report summarised his contribution in this way:

"He brought fresh ideas, wise counsel and friendly guidance to all facets of our
work. When advice was sought, when advice was needed, Cornock–Taylor gave
considered judgement with simplicity and sincerity whether the matter was
of little or of great importance. His quality of leadership through convincing
friendliness for every club and every boy endeared him to all, and we have good
cause to be grateful and pay tribute to a man of vigour who has knitted us more
closely together and shown us the real purpose and value of being members of
the Fed."

He was succeeded by P. Winterforde–Young in September 1956.

It seemed, however, that the stability earned by any new financial initiative was soon unsettled by new pressures. In the mid–1950s, rising maintenance costs and increasing fuel charges led to an uncertain and troubled outlook. The 1955–56 annual report considered the implications of these adverse 'winds':

"The Fed is conscious that these winds without windfalls may mean the
curtailment of our present development plans to establish boys' clubs where
they are needed on housing estates. Similarly, it will prove increasingly difficult
for many management committees of clubs to implement the salary scales for

full–time trained leaders recommended by the Fed last May after most careful consideration. This could mean that leaders will either carry on as best they can with inadequate salaries for full–time work, or they will be forced to turn from their vocation in fairness to their families.

An alternative is to provide a strong cadre of trained part–time leaders. The Fed is already exploring that avenue, for we are fully aware that those in the past who could spare the time and had the personal means to do this vital work in a purely voluntary capacity are strictly limited in numbers today. The demand for leaders continues to increase, however, yet the urgency to help adolescent boys is far more difficult to accept today because the need is no longer an obvious physical one."

4. The Era of Expansion, the 1960s and 1970s

The Albemarle Committee, appointed in 1958 and reporting its findings on the future of the Youth Service in 1960, met at a time when there was a feeling that adolescent independence as expressed through an emerging teenage culture was beginning to collide with adult authority. The Albemarle Committee's view of the stability of society was almost as fearful and uncertain as that of the Victorian philanthropists. The Report articulates its apprehensiveness about the restiveness of youth by referring to the bulge in the adolescent population and the ending of national service as 'emergencies'. The Committee clearly believed that the 'freeing' of large numbers of young people on the population would 'strain' the Youth Service, unless it could find ways of diverting this 'considerable surplus energy'. These concerns about a new social phenomenon were accentuated by the increase in the rates of juvenile delinquency It was this sense of turbulence which prompted the Committee to ask if this crime wave might be associated with disturbed social conditions. Though it suspended judgement on this question, it expressed its disquiet about the effect of these new social pressures on the order and discipline of the existing world:

> *"One thing is sure–in the next few years young people will be entering employment in conditions of change and flexibility which will add to the strains of adolescence and the problems of adjustment to the adult world." ('The Youth Service in England and Wales', Albemarle, 1960.)*

The adult view of the social climate in the 1950s was that it was marked by the increasing influence of youth and a correspondingly growing hostility on the part of young people to established convention and traditional authority. Christopher Booker summed up the new spirit in these terms:

> *"To some of the older and more established sections of the community, this new force, with its enviously institutionalised forms of rebellion, its declarations of moral emancipation, its search for 'kicks' (and the first stories of drug taking in Soho coffee bars) admittedly seemed positively threatening. Certainly, nobody could deny the increase which had taken place since 1956 in every form of youthful crime and violence." ('The Neophiliacs', Christopher Booker, 1969.)*

The Albemarle Committee recognised, in its chapter on 'The World of Young People', that adolescence is always a period of conflict between the energies of growing individuals and the established customs of adult society. But it also felt that major social changes left the individual even more exposed to strain and disturbance than would normally be the case during adolescence, 'the most disturbed period of their lives'. Young people, within this analysis of social change and adolescent development, are seen to be 'puzzled', 'unsure' and 'sometimes ready to express their uncertainty in strange or even violent forms'. After the collective experience of the war years, there was a sense of a new point of departure for the Youth Service and the role of young people within it. This sense, Frank Dawes claims, was reinforced as the original public school educated leaders and supporters of the clubs died or retired:

"But now their creed was out of date; a creed based on the interpretation of the Christian ethic which emphasised loyalty, honour, duty and obedience; a creed which embodied the Winchester College motto 'Manners Makyth Man'. As one of the new leaders, Richard O'Brien, wrote in 'The Boy', in the spring of 1947: 'They have stamped the Service of Youth with their own design, and we who follow after must conform. Can we fit in easily? Is our attitude the same as theirs was yesterday? Questions such as these are now being asked in many clubs up and down the country. In the first place, we come from a very different background. We grew up in the period between the two wars. We were, if anything, iconoclasts; we abandoned the old beliefs in King and Country, noblesse oblige, and (often) in God himself. We do not feel competent to teach a code because we are not so certain that we are qualified to be proved inheritors of a glorious past, but rather we regard ourselves as involved with the rest of mankind in its struggle to find an answer to the problems of the present. Do manners makyth man? Might they just as easily mar man if taught in the wrong way against an unfamiliar background?" ('A Cry from the Streets: The Boys' Club Movement in Britain from the 1850s to the Present Day', Frank Dawes, 1975.)*

This kind of statement was symbolic of an accelerating trend in the post-war years to mark a distance between a newly emerging Youth Service and the philanthropic motivations of the early founders of the youth work and their consolidators in the 1920s and 1930s, who emphasised 'government under direction and leadership'.

Yet the Albemarle Committee did recognise that the Youth Service needed to be modernised, both in the buildings in which it operated and in its modus operandi. It put forward the case for an ambitious expansion programme; recommended that local education authorities should make capital grants, and give increased revenue support, to voluntary organisations; and encouraged the establishment of an emergency training college to increase the number of full-time leaders from 700 to 1,300 by 1966. The Albemarle Report ushered in what Bernard Davies describes as a 'golden age':

"If the youth service ever had a golden age, then the 1960s was certainly it ... Over the decade the service really did experience steady and sometimes heady expansion—more money, buildings and equipment, increased support for the voluntary sector, extra staff and training opportunities, better flows of information and publicity." ('From Voluntaryism to Welfare State: A History of the Youth Service in England' Vol 1, Bernard Davies, 1999.)*

The Federation shared this growing sense in the late–1950s and 1960s that the nation was entering a period of change in its social and cultural life and that it too must adapt to the changing scene. It acknowledged that the circumstances of boys had greatly changed in the previous ten years, and that their attitudes, tastes and habits were changing as a result·

"The vastly improved conditions at home, at school and at work, together with easily obtained recreations and increased spending power, are making boys very selective of leisure time pursuits... It is obvious that our future methods, our club buildings and our leadership must be far more inspiring if we are to guide and help boys when they turn to our clubs for personal friendship."

In the spring of 1957, a Commission on Boys' Club Work was appointed, chaired by Judge Aarvold, to conduct a general review of the Federation's work, with a brief 'to examine and advise on the function of boys' clubs and the Federation in present–day society'.

The report was completed in December 1958 and affirmed in its conclusions the continuing value of boys' clubs:

> *"We regard the continued existence and provision of boys' clubs in the London area as being a matter not only of great importance to the boys in a particular area, but one of vital importance to London as well. In the conditions that obtain in London today, and which are likely to continue, it is essential that places such as clubs should be available where boys can spend their leisure time and youthful exuberance of spirit in a positive way under first class guidance."*

But its specific recommendations related less to youth work issues and more to organisational changes, which the Federation was not always prepared to accept. For example, Aarvold recommended that the Fed should 'become a central authority in control of the boys' clubs in the area'. But the Federation felt that such centralisation would jeopardise the local roots of the movement. Aarvold also suggested some degree of streamlining and decentralisation. The Federation's Executive was not prepared to delegate its administration to separate geographical areas, though it did ask the NABC to investigate the possibility of establishing a separate organisation for Middlesex (this proposal was subsequently implemented). Aarvold also recommended that the Fed should concentrate on the over–14s and cease its work with under–14s. The Federation decided to defer any decision on this matter. It did accede to the proposal to channel the many duties of the Executive through six standing committees and two panels. It was also agreed to add two new posts to the establishment–an Activities Officer and a Recruitment/Training Officer – though Aarvold's recommendation that a Public Relations Officer should be appointed was not pursued.

In many ways, the Federation was well equipped to consolidate and expand its work at the time of the Aarvold Commission. Its central staff consisted of 17 full–timers and 10 part–timers responsible for the work of Headquarters, Woodrow High House, and the Bellingham and Eltham sports grounds. 226 clubs were in membership, serviced by 81 full–time leaders, 36 part–time paid leaders and 100 voluntary leaders, 1,017 voluntary helpers and 332 paid instructors. Of the 226 clubs, 108 met on five or more nights of the week and 36 on four nights. 117 clubs had their own premises, 51 met in rented halls and 58 made use of schools.

In the late 1950s, the Federation was also attempting to revivify and diversify its activities. It was keen to find ways of integrating its Patron's Award Scheme into the programmes of the clubs. Progress was initially 'slow but sure':

> *"The flexible pattern of activities provided by the Duke of Edinburgh's Award Scheme is acknowledged by all to be extremely valuable, but up to the present time this scheme appears to be attracting only a limited number of club boys, although many clubs are tending to use the scheme as a blueprint for their programmes, even though the members do not enter the scheme."*

By 1959, however, 28 clubs were participating in the scheme. The Federation continued to introduce more flexibility, imagination and challenge into the programme offer: rural expeditions, gliding, rock climbing, pot-holing and shark fishing were some of the more adventurous activities offered as a way of injecting a greater degree of challenge:

"Although many do so, there are still far too many clubs which rely on dull, stereotyped programmes that provide insufficient challenge to today's club members."

So successful was this diversification of activity that the Fed was able to report in 1964–65 that, for the first time ever, projects had been offered and undertaken on every weekend of the year. On the cultural side, an Arts Festival was convened, and debates, drama and music were given a new focus.

The organisation's capacity to provide a wide range of activities to its membership was enhanced in 1964 by its acquisition of Hindleap Warren. Over 350 acres of forest land in Ashdown Forest was leased, at a peppercorn rent, by the Manor Charitable Trust to the Fed to be used for a projects centre and as a base for the Duke of Edinburgh's Award Scheme. Much of the initial work in adapting the site was carried out by club members:

"Roads were relaid by boys during many weekends under wintry conditions, and by the New Year (1965) many drainage systems had been dug. Boys camped throughout the winter months, sometimes in deep snow, and it was during these periods that inter–site telephones were laid, working huts reconstructed, six camping site areas cleared and bench seats and open fire places built."

At this stage, Hindleap was essentially a camp site. 10 sites with log cabins were established, each one catering for 50 boys with its own water supply and sanitation.

The addition of Hindleap did not lead to the neglect of the Federation's existing training centre at Woodrow High House. By 1966, 3,500 adults, boys and girls were using the centre. A major development scheme was launched in 1964, incorporating roof repairs, rewiring, new staff houses, the building of a new wing and gymnasium, and the modernisation and re–equipment of the kitchen. The main contributors to the financing of the scheme were the Department of Education and Science and the Worshipful Company of Goldsmiths.

Significant changes emanated from the Development Committee, one of the standing committees recommended by Aarvold. It set itself the demanding but vital task of establishing new clubs at a time when few external sponsors took the first steps of pioneering new provision:

"A major responsibility of the Development Committee is the establishment of new clubs where they are needed. This is a relatively new branch of the Fed's work, for it will be remembered that the Fed grew up because existing clubs asked for membership. In recent times, however, it has become necessary for the Fed to initiate clubs where they are desperately needed but no spontaneous effort has been made to find and possibly acquire premises which are suitable for development as a Boys' Club; to recruit responsible men and women to serve on the adult committee of management; to find a leader and helpers; and to give the new organisation a start."

Accordingly, the Development Committee put in place a five year plan to set up 20 new clubs at a possible cost of £200,000, to be called 'The 20 Clubs Fund'. The areas selected (10 to the north of the river, and 10 in the south of London) were parts of the capital where the Federation had little or no presence. The early development of the organisation was associated with central areas–such as Bermondsey, Stepney, St Pancras and Westminster. The new policy was to extend the Fed's provision to the outer circle of Inner London–Greenwich, Wandsworth, Lewisham and Haringey.

This ambitious initiative demanded access to new sources of funding. This search was assisted by a grant from the King George's Fund to the NABC to allow it to second two full–time members of staff to help the Fed develop the new boys' clubs. The pattern of funding these new clubs was to seek multiple donations, but to associate a particular private donor or charity with each project. Thus, the Variety Club was the major benefactor of six–Streatham, Loughborough Junction, Grove Park, Harringay, Roehampton and Battersea Park–of the initial 13 developments. Leading contributors to the Variety Club's sponsorship were well known businessmen and impresarios, such as Sir Isaac Wolfson, Charles Clore, Jack Cotton, Sam Spiegel and Billy Butlin. Bellingham was sponsored by the Dulverton Trust and St Giles, Camberwell by the Pilgrim Trust. The largest sum of £50,000 (most of the contributions ranged from £5,000 to £26,000, £97,500 and £507,000 at current prices respectively) was given by the directors of the merchant bankers, Samuel Montagu and Company, to establish the Samuel Montagu Boys' Club in Kidbrooke.

Samuel Montagu Boys' Club opened in 1963, the largest of the 20 Clubs Main Building. East Elevation.

All of the projects were underpinned by grants of 50% from the Ministry of Education (later the Department of Education and Science) and grants of 25% from the LCC (later the ILEA), as a consequence of the first Youth Service capital building programme announced by the Government.

The first of the new generation of clubs–the Southfield Boys' Club in Wandsworth–was opened in October 1960, and all the schemes were finally completed by 1970, the last including Roehampton, Samuel Lithgow, Hollington, Battersea Park and Lewisham (the final one to open its doors in August 1970). But this major initiative did not bring to an end the Federation's commitment to a process of renewal and modernisation. A plan to improve and modernise 30 existing clubs constituted a key element in the 1966 Appeal. When the appeal was officially launched at a reception at Buckingham Palace, £200,000 had already been received or promised.

The Federation's efforts in the late 1950s to plan the building of new clubs and to make its programmes more attractive anticipated the recommendations of the Albemarle Report, which later argued a similar case for a major building programme on a national scale. The report also gave momentum to the move towards a closer partnership between the statutory and voluntary sectors. At the AGM in 1960, William Houghton, the Education Officer of the LCC, outlined the new LCC plan for youth work and affirmed its complementarity with the work of existing boys' clubs.

The Albemarle Report also emphasised the importance of training. It advocated the need for an increase in the number of trained leaders, and the Federation applauded this recommendation. It expressed its concern in 1964, however, that the number of newly trained leaders was in practice insufficient to meet the needs of the developing Youth Service. It traced the main reason for this to the high cost of housing in the capital. The Fed, in typical pragmatic mode, moved beyond a recognition of the problem to a search for a solution. It decided to acquire a property in Barnes Common, which was converted into flats to accommodate some of its full–time club leaders. £20,000 was made available by the 1966 Appeal, supported by a grant from the London Parochial Charities. Clubs, such as Devas, Stowe, Rugby and Poplar, took their own initiatives in building flats on the club premises for their staff. The Federation, during this period of development, was guided by its Chairman, Raymond Plummer, who had lived at the Oxford and Bermondsey settlement after graduating from Oxford and was closely associated with Westminster House Boys' Club in Nunhead (set up by his old school, Westminster).

The new climate also led the Federation to re–examine its attitude to the presence of girls in boys' clubs, prompted by the publication in 1962 of the NABC's booklet, 'Boys' Clubs in the Sixties'. The Federation's own rather lukewarm conclusion, declared in March 1963, was that 'providing boys' activities were safeguarded and proper arrangements and conditions made, there are occasions when girls should be welcomed into Boys' Clubs'. But it continued to regard its focus on boys as its priority:

> *"Boys' clubs have a particular responsibility for boys and great care must be taken to ensure that too rapid development of mixed activities does not seriously hinder the normal boys' activities."*

The Fed also considered its stance on 'single activity clubs'. Previously, it had held doubts about whether such units (like boxing clubs) should be affiliated. It now took a decision that provisional membership should be granted to specialist groups, 'subject to the understanding that such groups will, within 18 months of the granting of provisional membership, and with the assistance of the Fed, qualify as recognised Boys' Clubs'.

The Federation, recognising that it could no longer draw on men from the universities and public schools to act as volunteers in its clubs, looked instead to senior members who had grown up in the clubs and were searching for opportunities to become club leaders. New routes were opening up for them at the new National College at Leicester (the outcome of the Albemarle Committee's advocacy of an emergency training college) and at the NABC's Liverpool training centre. In November 1963, the Duke of Edinburgh extended the appeal for volunteers to the wider population of London:

> *"I believe there are hundreds, perhaps even thousands, of Londoners who would like to do something positive for the younger generation. I can assure them from personal experience that there is nothing more positive than a Boys' Club. More adult helpers are needed in every area of London."*

Within a year, the Fed reported a considerable increase in the number of Londoners volunteering their services. An advertising campaign in the London press produced over 100 voluntary helpers.

The Fed also reviewed its age groups, which had remained defiantly at 14 to 18 since its origins (though under–14 clubs had been introduced as a concession to a younger clientele). It decided in 1964–65 to lower the age limit of the main section of clubs to 13 and to raise the upper age limit to 19. The decision was accompanied by an admission that some clubs had already been practising for some time what the report recommended!

The Federation was determined to expand its activities despite continuing financial pressures:

> *"In spite of the deficit (£11,065 in 1965) and rising costs, the Fed feels that it must continue to do everything possible to expand its existing services to satisfy the rapidly growing demand from its affiliated clubs. The scale and scope of the Fed's activities continue to increase, and during the year a further revision and increase in staff salaries took place."*

The expansion of activities in this period is exemplified by the Devas's involvement in a multiplicity of initiatives in the summer of 1968: a canoeing trip from Southampton to the Isle of Wight; canoe surfing at Camber Sands; a fishing trip to the Norfolk Broads; a fortnight's annual holiday, one week in the Lake District and one week in North Wales; and a weekend expedition on Viscount Amory's sloop, 'Ailanthus', on the Solent. The club's enduring association with University College, Oxford also continued to be expressed by football and cricket fixtures between the club and the college, and the involvement of Masters of the college–including Lord Goodman, Lord Redcliffe–Maude and Lord Butler–as trustees. The expansion of the Federation's work led it to move into new premises at 121 Kennington Park Road, after a 38 year stay at 222 Blackfriars Road.

The Federation felt the need to reiterate the value of its work in the 1960s under the leadership of Bill Rice, who became General Secretary in 1960, when the behaviour of groups of young people was becoming to be perceived as a social problem. The Federation's new President, Viscount Amory (who, as Derick Heathcote–Amory, had been Chancellor of the Exchequer from 1958 to 1960), reaffirmed the organisation's relevance in this changing social context:

> *"There are many people today who, because of the extravagances and misbehaviour of a minority of young people, are feeling somewhat disenchanted with 'youth'. Unfortunately, the decent behaviour of the majority is not news. Perhaps the fact that it is not, because it is normal, is something to rejoice in. It is our job to convince those who have lost faith in youth to keep a fair perspective. Whether we like the idea or not, the generation growing up is going to be in charge of the nation's affairs within a very few years. It, therefore, must be right to do all we can to give them an opportunity for wholesome, positive, worthwhile interests and activities during their impressionable years."*

He stressed that the only limitations to the organisation's rate of advance were the practical ones of leadership and finance.

1965 Arts Festival, held at the Brady Club.

The effort to provide 'positive and worthwhile interests' did become news around this time, when the Evening Standard published an article which tried to capture the mood of a typical club:

> *"The Vallance Boys' Club in Chicksand Street, Whitechapel, has a reputation for toughness. I had heard club leaders speak of it with mingled awe and apprehension. I expected a Fagin's den and certainly, as I approached it one dark and stormy night, the shadowy figures in black leather jackets and winklepickers larking in the doorways of Chicksand Street seemed to confirm this expectation. Later I discovered that these were teenagers who were trying to join the club, but had had to be turned away because it was full. It was dance night. Lights were low in the big room, and the boxing ring in the corner and the baulks of timber supporting the sagging ceiling gave the club an air of drama. At first the girls were jiving together, then the boys began to lose their shyness and join in. But mostly the boys–three Cypriots from Famagusta, market boys from Petticoat Lane, office boys from the furniture factories of Shoreditch and the Stepney breweries–stood about in groups, relaxed and smiling, not talking much, but tapping their tapered shoes to the beat.*
>
> *Tom Derby is the club leader. He is a clothing salesman by day, he has a London accent and he fits easily into the club scene. The boys call him 'Tom'. There are two dance nights a week when they can bring girls. Otherwise they concentrate on sports and games, particularly boxing and football. Probably the Vallance Boys' Club has no particular educational value. Certainly it does not try to influence the religious or political thoughts of the boys. There are no strings attached. It helps its members to amuse themselves and keeps them off street corners and out of dockland cafes. It is the sort of club the East End desperately needs. It is a true club and, in its way, is as successful as White's."*

The Fed highlighted the continuing and vital role of the voluntary youth club of this kind in its response to the ILEA's Review of Youth and Adult Services:

> *"We intend to continue to provide what we believe to be what the majority of young men want and need in this day of the so–called 'permissive society'– positive and sensitive leadership and purposeful activity based on the friendly atmosphere of a good club where men extend to boys aspiring to manhood the valuable gifts of friendship and understanding. Our continuing need is for men and money to invest in this great enterprise."*

The local education authority was in this decade a major 'investor' in the enterprise. The Federation first received a grant from the LCC towards its administrative costs in 1961–62, and the grant increased every year. In 1966, the grant of £4,900 towards its central costs formed an 'irreplaceable' part of the organisation's income. The LCC also made a grant of £800 to Woodrow High House in 1961, in addition to its capital grants to the 20 Clubs. From 1962, individual clubs were also benefiting from its increasingly generous financial support. As well as salary grants (not exceeding 75%) for full–time and part time leaders, clubs received an annual maintenance grant (not exceeding 25%) towards approved items of maintenance expenditure, such as rent, rates, heating and lighting. Capital grants (not exceeding 25%) were available towards the cost of providing new or improved premises, and special grants were offered for a variety of purposes, such as experimental work, the purchase of vehicles and extraordinary items of maintenance expenditure.

The extent of grant-aid from the LCC was indicative of a strengthening relationship between the statutory authority and the voluntary youth sector. One of the last reports of the LCC, before the Inner London Education Authority (ILEA) took over its educational functions in 1964 as part of a London–wide local government reorganisation, was unequivocal about the importance of this partnership:

> *"In the development of the Youth Service over the last quarter of a century, the LCC has succeeded in establishing a partnership with the voluntary bodies in London. 3,000 voluntary youth groups of various kinds exist in the inner London area, many attached to the London branches of national voluntary youth organisations, and a fair number of them receive assistance from the Council. It has been the LCC's endeavour to work in close co–operation with these voluntary organisations, to offer facilities for classes and instructors, to furnish technical advice and, latterly, to prepare an annual building programme for the provision of accommodation for youth clubs and youth centres."*

The Youth Service Development Council's working party, chaired by Fred Milson and Andrew Fairbairn, was responsible in 1969 for the publication of 'Youth and Community Work in the 70s', which advocated an uncompromising policy of encouraging young people to play an active part in society. It stressed the importance of participation, pressing for a greater element of self–determination by young people at the expense of adult direction of the service. The Milson–Fairbairn Committee's support for what it called the 'active society' was based on its recognition of the reality of a quickly changing society and its openness to the potential benefits of change and adaptation. Whereas the Albemarle Report seemed to regret that there was no longer a consensus in society, 'Youth and Community Work in the 70s' positively embraced change. It accepted the transformation of society as a fact of life, as an inevitable consequence of a modern technological society:

> *"In a country such as ours, subject to changes consequent upon a rapidly developing technology, society needs to engage in an intensive and perpetual transformation of itself, unless it is to respond to tomorrow's world with yesterday's activities and modes of organisation. Our commitment is to a society in which every member can be publicly active, for only in this way can society become positively responsible to them and, in the constant renewal of itself, reflect their values." ('Youth and Community Work in the 70s', Youth Service Development Council, 1969.)*

The openness and responsiveness of the report were a reflection of the hope and optimism of the decade of the 1960s. Optimistic that a society 'In which all can make more and more decisions about more and more things' was attainable, the Council's report entertained no reservations that young people possessed the capacities of awareness and responsibility to play an active part in this evolving society. While previous commentators had seen the inexperience and confusion of young people as a brake on their full involvement and participation, this report saw their lack of experience as a positive advantage:

"The young have the energy and aspirations untrammelled by past failure to secure some parts of the transformation of society which elders are not necessarily better qualified to achieve."

Where the Albemarle Report was ambivalent about the adult status of young people, the Milson–Fairbairn Report unequivocally accepted their level of sophistication and supported their right to have a choice of their own.

In making sense of the notion of participation in an active society, the Council wrote of young people actively 'creating', 'moulding' and 'shaping' the society in which they lived.

Its concept of youth work represented a clear distinction from the preservation of the status quo of the Nineteenth Century pioneers and the assumption of adolescent self–determination within the confirmation of existing values and institutions preferred by the Albemarle Committee:

"We are not so much concerned today as in the past with basic education, or with economic needs, or with the communication of a grand belief or value system, but we are concerned to help young people to create their place in a changing society and it is their critical involvement in their community which is the goal."

The influence of the Milson–Fairbairn Report was such that by the early 1970s youth work had become youth and community work, setting youth work within the context of community development and making a contribution to a more participative democracy.

The Federation did not respond so favourably to 'Youth and Community Work in the 70s' as it had done to the Albemarle Report in 1960. Its immediate comment was terse:

"We do not wish to comment on this report other than to say that it does not in our view give proper recognition to the indispensable role of the voluntary worker in the Youth Service without whom the present level of activity could not be maintained, and nothing that it says affects our judgement that the work of the Boys' Clubs in London is as vital today as in the past."

If it refrained from giving any serious consideration to 'Youth and Community Work in the 70s', the Federation felt sufficiently challenged by some of the new directions in youth work championed by Milson and Fairbairn-detached youth work, community-based youth work-to articulate a rationale of its work in changing circumstances as a centrepiece of its 1970–71 annual report:

"Times have changed. Conditions of work, education and housing for many, but not all, have been revolutionised. The modern boy commands purchasing power, mobility and opportunities undreamed of by the boys who made up the membership of the handful of clubs who formed the Fed in 1887.

Times have changed too for the management and leadership of our clubs. Today 67 of our affiliated clubs employ professional leaders. These men, and many of the part–time and voluntary leaders, are trained and are properly recognised as important social workers. At their disposal is an ever increasing volume of research, writings and advice which was certainly not available to their early predecessors. This professional approach is to be welcomed and encouraged to the end that the standard of the work is improved and the understanding of the young advanced."

Though sceptical of the relevance of 'Youth and Community Work in the 70s' to its work, the Federation accepted the need to re-examine its impact by undertaking another review. It reduced its committees from 13 to six: Action, Finance, Club Services, Sports, Training and Activities. The hope was that the time that had previously been spent 'in committee' would now be more profitably spent in servicing member clubs. In that change of emphasis, the role of Club Services became more prominent. Though officers gave support to clubs experiencing difficulties, their priority was to visit all member clubs on a regular basis, acting as the 'eyes and ears' of the Fed.

The Federation was in a relatively secure financial position during the 1970s. In the 1972–73 annual report, it was able to report that its deficit of £3,534 was the lowest for very many years, and the balance of its capital fund had increased by £22,607, despite the inflationary pressures of the times. The main supporters continued to be the ILEA, the NABC, Goldsmiths and the City Parochial Foundation. In 1972–73, Club Week generated a new record of £15,223. At the same time, steady income from the Boys' Club Shop was beginning to dry up. In 1966–67, it had made a profit of £5,984, but in 1970–71 it made no profit, and in 1971–72 the Fed needed to make a grant of £1,932 to cover its deficit.

In 1972, the Duke of Edinburgh was awarded the Sir Charles Wrench Memorial Medallion in recognition of his 25 years as Patron. During that time, the hallmark of his tenure was his frequent tours of Federation clubs. In May 1960, for example, he opened the new building of the Brady Club in Spitalfields, and went on to the Lion Boys' Club in Hoxton, where he was shown the plans of its projected new premises. On all these occasions, he showed a real ability to establish a cheerful rapport with the young people themselves, rather than restrict himself to staider conversations with the adult leaders and supporters.

Clubs were the grateful beneficiaries of a revised scheme of grant aid introduced by the ILEA in 1972. Salary grants for youth workers were increased from 75% to 100%, and voluntary organisations were given the option of their leaders being appointed by the Authority and then seconded to the organisation, an option that reduced the administrative burden on clubs. Grant aid on maintenance items was increased from 25% to 50%, though on a narrower range of items, and the system of claiming the grant was simplified. The ILEA was remarkably sensitive to the financial vulnerability of voluntary organisations, as its annual report for 1974–75 shows:

"The Youth Service has traditionally been a developing partnership between voluntary and statutory agencies, and this close relationship is fully reflected in the composition of youth committees, both centrally and at local level. We have therefore been particularly concerned and distressed over the course of the year under review to see voluntary organisations at all levels coming under increasing financial pressure. The membership of voluntary organisations far exceeds that of statutory provision. These organisations rely upon charitable funds to supplement grant-aid received from the Authority and they have found it increasingly difficult to raise such funds. Few, if any, have reserves to fall back on and the alternative to closure of some will be increased grant-aid.

The Duke of Edinburgh visits the Devas Club in 1963

The contribution that the voluntary organisations make to the Youth Service in London must be stressed. They raise large sums of money for themselves, but more important, to supplement the paid leadership the Authority provides, they raise a large number of voluntary youth workers without whom the service could not operate.

The picture that has emerged has been of organisations delaying or postponing salary increases for their staff (other than those 100% grant-aided by the Authority), who consequently fall behind their colleagues undertaking comparable work elsewhere; organisations generally are facing reduced income from charitable and other sources, as benefactors themselves come under pressure from the inflationary spiral; and there have been cut–backs in existing provision as well as hopes and plans for the future. Indeed, as the year covered by this report ends, we are aware of a significant number of applications from voluntary organisations for special deficit grants which we will shortly have to consider."

Though the Federation clearly benefited from the ILEA's generous financial support, it remained a little defensive in the face of what it saw as a potential threat to its independence from the expanding statutory service. In the 1973–74 annual report, it felt the need to register its separateness and distinctiveness:

"No local education authority could say that boys' clubs could be replaced by statutory services. The facts are that the greater part of the Youth Service is dependent upon thousands of voluntary workers and voluntary funds, without which the whole service would collapse. Despite generous financial support from the London education authority, figures show that in Fed clubs £60 has to be found from voluntary services, including the members' own efforts, for every £40 received in grant-aid... The danger of attempting to be all things to all men is, however, a very real one. Men and women working in boys' clubs are inevitably concerned for the young casualties of our modern materialistic society. The victims of drug addiction, drink, homelessness and violence challenge the conscience of all responsible people. There is, however, a great temptation to undertake responsibility for areas of work for which one may not be equipped or for which resources are inadequate. Alongside these pressures are those from the enthusiastic experimenters, who are happy to put at risk or reject worthwhile work, often in over-publicised or ill-judged attempts to reach the many unattached young people. The Youth Service like many other areas of social and educational work is suffering from a surfeit of experts, consultants and observers and a dearth of men and women who will get on with it."

This defiant message, while distancing the Fed from the 'enthusiastic experimenters' of the post–Milson and Fairbairn era, was also intended to highlight its practical approach to 'getting on with the job'. It maintained that boys' clubs were not first–aid agencies concerned only with young people in trouble, but with 'ordinary young people, many of whom are underprivileged due to circumstances beyond their control'. It returned to this theme in the 1974–75 annual report, perhaps feeling that 'ordinary' work was undervalued within a fast–moving and multi–layered Youth Service:

"The work we do rarely attracts the headlines. Pop Festivals, juvenile crime, anti–social behaviour all receive massive publicity and some may think a disproportionate amount of time, energy and scarce resources. We neglect at our peril the kind of youngsters who make up the majority of the Fed's membership."

Yet, despite the Fed's wish to detach itself from what it saw as 'over–publicised and ill–judged' attempts to respond to the wider aspirations encouraged by the Milson–Fairbairn Report, it did broaden the scope of its work and make its own contribution to the changing priorities of youth work. It took some pride in reporting in 1974 that several clubs were heavily involved in community projects. Club premises were extensively used for old people's welfare, school meals, playgroups and holiday projects. In 1976, it started its first Job Creation Programme, giving temporary employment to a team of unemployed young men who assisted in the repair and redecoration of clubs. By the end of the year, through this scheme, four members had been placed in permanent employment and two had gone on to further education. In the face of increasing unemployment, many clubs were helping their members to find work by contacting employers, preparing them for interviews and encouraging them to undertake further vocational training. It was the first youth organisation to appoint a full–time Environmental Services Officer as a response to the interest in wildlife stimulated by residential stays at Woodrow High House. A number of boys under intermediate treatment orders (a community–based approach to the rehabilitation of young offenders) attended courses at Woodrow and Hindleap.

The Finals of the Federation's Junior Quiz Competition, 1972

Within its own terms, the Federation continued to build on its successes. The highlight of 1975 was the opening of the Bernard Sunley Activity Centre at Hindleap at a cost of £300,000 (the equivalent today of about £2,130,000), providing permanent facilities to replace the original camps. The Fed, through the generosity of the Worshipful Company of Goldsmiths, obtained the use of an additional playing field in Acton, a useful balance in the west of London to the grounds in the south east.

Eight of the Federation's full-time youth leaders, in post but unqualified, were accepted on to the ILEA's newly introduced qualification course at Avery Hill College. Further discussions took place to increase the organisation's participation in the Duke of Edinburgh's Award Scheme. During this period, clubs were supported by a Senior Training Officer, three Club Services Officers (who made more than 1,000 visits to clubs in the year) and a Sports Officer. An Arts Service team, with a full-time officer for the first time, made over 50 demonstration visits to member clubs a year.

The revamped Hindleap Warren is officially opened by the Duke of Edinburgh in 1976

5. The Era of Uncertainty, 1976–1998

The early years of the 1970s witnessed in many ways a continuation of the upsurge during the 1960s of the interest in involving young people in decision-making processes. But the economic difficulties of the decade, as the oil-price crisis of 1973 was followed by serious inflationary pressures, began to reveal social tensions, which seemed to demonstrate the increasing difficulty of holding together British society as a cohesive whole. The optimism of the 1960s gave way to the disillusionment of the 1970s, and Harold Haywood contrasted the way in which young people had gained a sense of power and liberation in the 1960s to the way in which that power ebbed away in the 1970s:

> *"There is no doubt that the 60s was a lynchpin decade. It gave power into the hands of the people and particularly to young people. The 70s have seen an ebbing of that power, since the economic forces of a recession and vast unemployment have taken away from young people the opportunity to make money by work, even on a casual basis." ('Where Are They Now?', Harold Hayward, 1977.)*

The economic pressures also began to expose the youth sector to cuts, as Bernard Davies points out:

> *"Economic policies, sometimes though not always driven by economic downturn, squeezed public expenditure generally. For the youth service this initially meant standstill budgets at best and cuts in planned growth. In the later years of the decade, repeating waves of real and often very harsh cuts again in effect reduced the service to non–statutory status within local provision as local authorities chose to fund it (or not) at highly unpredictable and variable levels." ('From Thatcherism to New Labour: A History of the Youth Service' Vol 2, Bernard Davies, 1999.)*

In this worsening social and economic context, the Fed was compelled to weather the economic storms prevalent at the time. In March 1974, it recorded its smallest deficit (£2,232) for many years, but it was at pains to explain that 'the present rate of inflation will certainly mean a much more serious deficit next year'. Indeed, the deficit did increase to over £15,000 by March 1975. It set its own financial problems, however, in the context of the national economic travails:

> *"The future of the country is uncertain and fraught with difficulties and to refer to our financial problems may seem hardly relevant."*

The Federation was also concerned about the social problems that accompanied the economic crisis, as it declared in the 1975–76 annual report:

> *"Society is very properly concerned about juvenile crime and unemployment among the young. The Fed shares that concern and, whilst believing that the resolving of these problems is largely dependent upon economic and social factors outside its province, we believe we are making a contribution to at least moderating their effect on the lives of our members."*

The Fed was helped to emerge from the financial crisis by a new appeal, launched at Buckingham Palace on 14 June 1977. In connection with the launch of this appeal, the Duke of Edinburgh visited three clubs in South London, including the Devas:

> *"The Duke of Edinburgh wound up the evening with an extended tour of Devas. On arrival, the Warden (Steve Sipple) and members of the Council of Management were presented by the Chairman, Mr W.A. Mackenzie. The Warden then accompanied HRH on a tour of the club, presented instructors, helpers and members. The Duke visited every corner of the club and showed a keen interest in the activities in progress."*

A large proportion of the money raised was to be allocated to the improvement of club premises and the development of new facilities for the 161 clubs (and over 18,000 young people) in membership. The continuing take-up of the Fed's offer is demonstrated by the remarkable fact that, of those 161 clubs, 140 were open on three nights a week (of these, 83 were open on five or more nights). 5,500 boys from 118 clubs participated in sports and competitions. 1,142 members from 94 clubs were involved in training, the arts and outdoor pursuits. £417,737 was eventually raised by the appeal, and the Fed was able to put in train 'Operation Lifeline', enabling the modernisation of a number of affiliated clubs, including new premises for Chelsea Boys' Club and an extension at Marvel Lane Boys' Club (one of the 20 Clubs). Other clubs to benefit were Senrab, Bradfield, Woodberry Down, Southfields, Lion, Lewisham, Tooting, Red Lion, North Paddington, Roehampton and Cameron Athan. A portion of the money was committed to the provision of a covered swimming pool at each of the training centres. A major donor to 'Operation Lifeline' was the Joseph Levy Foundation. Joe Levy had been a member and manager of the Brady Club and established the Foundation in 1965. The Foundation supported the Federation extensively in the latter decades of the Twentieth Century, particularly funding building projects and making Woodrow High House more accessible to young people with disabilities.

The organisation remained ambivalent, even suspicious, about the use of public funds for new, more radical initiatives, as this comment on political education in the 1978–79 annual report illustrates:

> *"Recently, public money has been allocated for the political education of the young and to alert them to their rights in society. There has been somewhat less emphasis on their responsibilities. We suggest that the training our members receive in a good Boys' Club covers this need at no extra cost to public funds."*

The Federation introduced 'The Five Year Plan' to meet the challenges of the 1980s. In many ways, the document was a restatement of the organisation's aims, residing its continuing trust in 'ordinary', club-based work. It clearly felt that club work was back in fashion, noting in the 1980–81 annual report that 'there has been a gradual and marked reversal back to the essentials of good club work, where challenging leadership, discipline, self-respect and a sense of responsibility are being upheld with immense success'. The new threat to its work was the cut-backs to public services implemented by the Thatcher Government:

> *"The Youth Service is faced with a real dilemma at this initial stage where limitation of the funds available often determine the nature and scope of the work which can be carried out. It would be irresponsible of the Fed if we did not advocate that further*

The launch of the Five Year Plan coincided with the appointment of Reynold 'Cass' Edwards as General Secretary. He had been the Fed's Sports Officer since 1974 (and, briefly, Deputy General Secretary). During that time, the annual report for 1978–79 recorded that 'he had developed a first class rapport with Fed clubs and the numerous members who entered the many sports events that are organised'. He carried over this natural and unrivalled ability to relate to young people in informal situations into his work as General Secretary. He replaced Alf Gibbs who had been General Secretary for 11 years from 1969 (he had previously been the NABC's Regional Officer for the West and the South–West). He had sought insistently to maintain the fundamental standards of youth work, as the annual report of 1979–80 underlined:

"His determination to have nothing to do with a slackening of standards did much to strengthen and extend the influence of the Boys' Club movement and the Fed in particular."

At the end of the decade, the Federation's offices in Kennington were named Wagg House in recognition of the generous support provided over the years by the Wagg family (A.R.Wagg had been joint Hon. Secretary from 1916 to 1918 and R.E.Wagg had been the Fed's Chair from 1971 to 1973).

The Five Year Plan was compatible with the latest national report on the Youth Service, the Thompson Report (published in 1982 as 'Experience and Participation'), in a way that the Fed never felt comfortable with the diagnosis and prognosis of the Milson–Fairbairn Report. The annual report of 1982–83 took reassurance from this convergence of objectives:

"The Fed believes that its present role and emphasis is both sensitive and appropriate to the changing needs and aspirations of young men growing up in a complex and ever changing environment with all its pressures and constraints. The recent publication of the Thompson Report, together with the clear objectives in our own Five Year Plan, incline us to believe that we are very much on the right course and an essential part of London's Youth Service."

The Thompson Report did not view social change in as confidently optimistic a way as the Milson–Fairbairn Report. It was as conscious as its precursor of the fact of rapid social change, but it saw losses as well as gains in this process. The experience of change presented particular problems and difficulties for young people:

"Against the positive features of modern society ...must be set a number of factors which are, to say the least, perplexing and confusing to adults, and which must seem all the more menacing to those who are still reaching out for a secure identity." ('Experience and Participation', Report of the Review of the Youth Service in England, 1982.)

Some of the factors which the Thompson Committee identified as increasing the pressures on young people were the decline of the family, an increasingly mobile society, a worsening of the quality of the environment, unemployment, racism and homelessness.

The Federation responded positively to many of the contemporary issues highlighted by the Thompson Report. It applauded the emphasis placed on the multi-ethnic dimension of youth work, noting that the ethnic mix in clubs was an important element of boys' club work. It accepted that priority should be given to measures to combat youth unemployment, though it added the qualifying statement that any intervention by the Fed should be complementary to the establishment of day-time provision by well-funded Government agencies. In relation to young people and the police, it professed its intention to continue to work towards improving trust between the law enforcement agencies and those who fell foul of the law. It was, however, more reserved in its response to the Thompson Report's accent on anti-sexist work, arguing that it was 'well aware that some young men, as do some young women, choose a single sex setting at certain stages in their development'.

The Government's legislation to limit public expenditure, however, continued to cause the Fed uncertainty and unease, as the annual report for 1983–84 made clear:

> "It is at times like these that those of us who work in the voluntary service
> of young people are made to feel vulnerable and certainly undervalued by a
> society which derives so much benefit from our efforts."

The Federation played an active role in the campaign to protect the voluntary youth organisations, even taking Peter Brooke MP, the Under–Secretary of State responsible for the Youth Service, on a tour of clubs. It used the occasion to argue that clubs were a cost–effective way of opening up beneficial opportunities for young people:

> "The Thompson Report set out the deficiencies in terms of the quantity and
> quality of existing Youth Service provision and practice. Few would argue
> that there is no room for improvement. There can, however, be few more cost–
> effective means of delivering such a range of services and opportunities than
> work undertaken by thousands of volunteers operating in numerous voluntary
> youth organisations which clearly benefit the thousands of young people who
> live and work in our capital city."

The Federation's contribution was vigorously supported by the London Youth Committee, which again registered in its 1986–87 annual report its appreciation of the role of the voluntary sector and its awareness of its particular vulnerability to the continuing financial restraints:

> "Social conditions within which the service was operating had become harsher.
> The growing financial restraints-already apparent in 1985–86-required
> allowing the service greater financial flexibility. The service's finances have
> become further constrained by the effects of decisions in previous years
> on capital commitments. The great value of the voluntary sector and its
> contribution to the service were recognised, as was its greater vulnerability to
> any reductions in grant-aid."

500 members take part in the Centenary Fun Run in Eastway

Despite the threat to its funding and an accompanying sense of vulnerability, the Federation celebrated its centenary in 1987 with confidence and optimism. In that year, it orchestrated a succession of prestigious and high profile celebration events–in February, a centenary banquet at the Guildhall was the setting to launch an appeal; in June, another banquet took place at Hampton Court; Westminster Abbey was the location of a dinner for representatives of the founding clubs; and a service of Thanksgiving and Rededication was held at St Paul's Cathedral. A group of club members went on a trip to Chicago and New York; a cricket team toured Barbados; a summer camp was organised in the South of France; and 500 members from 33 clubs participated in a special centenary fun run. At a special celebration at the St Andrew's Club, 30 past members were finally presented with medals that they been awarded during the Second World War. The shortage of metal because of the war effort had meant that the Federation was unable to give them to the winners at the time. The Fed looked back at its 100 years of achievement with a natural sense of pride:

"In 1987, the Fed reaches its one hundredth year in the service of London's youth. It is, therefore, timely for us to reflect on the pioneering work and remarkable vision of our philanthropic Victorian founders, who laid the foundations of what we have since come to regard as major social and welfare reforms. It was their passionate concern and resolute determination to improve the lives of the poor and particularly the young, which led to a systematic investigation into the full extent of the poverty which existed, with a real commitment to alleviate it...

*It may seem too hard for us to visualise the working boy in London a 100 years
ago, stunted or broken in the first years of a premature working life, driven to
the point of exhaustion or near collapse by unscrupulous employers who would
extend the working day at whim, without fear of detection or conscience.*

*Legislation and appropriate social provision, therefore, seemed the only hope
of ameliorating the squalor and hopelessness in which many found themselves,
and from which few could hope to escape–except for some to the temporary
haven of the club."*

To spur on its work for the next century, the Fed embarked on an ambitious appeal with a target
of £2 million. Some of the uses to which the money would be put focused on the continuation of
the Fed's most recent priorities–the building of new boys' clubs in designated areas of pressing
need; the modernisation and improvement of existing club buildings; and the recruitment and
training of more volunteers. Other proposed uses pointed the organisation in newer directions,
including the development of facilities for the disabled and the extension of the programme
for international contacts. But the most ground–breaking proposal was the development of
a Training, Arts and Employment Centre in Docklands, incorporating a training wing, a
youth employment workshop, an arts room and a canoe workshop. The success of the appeal
had increased the Federation's capital and reserves to £2,336,096 by 1991. Bridge House in
Docklands was acquired for £1,478,393, and the remainder of the appeal receipts were to be
used to complete the equipping of the new training and canoe facilities. The new Headquarters
was opened on 16 March 1990.

The success of the centenary year and the planned progress of the organisation in its aftermath
was, however, quickly disturbed by reports of further reductions from the ILEA and the
impending abolition of that body, as announced in the 1987–88 annual report:

*"The proposal to devolve the Education and Youth Service responsibility to the
remaining London Boroughs, and the constraints currently being placed on the
ILEA's expenditure, have created considerable uncertainty and anxiety in our clubs.
Voluntary workers and helpers who are already fully stretched are being asked to
accept further, significant reductions in funding and other vital resources, at a time
when the issues they must address are of increasing complexity."*

In fact, throughout the years of rate capping until its abolition in 1990, the ILEA gave
significant protection to the Youth Service and, particularly, the voluntary sector. The 50%
maintenance grant-aid scheme and the grant to the Federation as a headquarters organisation
remained unaffected during that time.

The value of the ILEA's support to youth work throughout London was fully acknowledged by
local clubs, as this appreciation by the Devas Club in its 1988–89 annual report proves:

*"This is not the place for a eulogy on the achievements of the ILEA, even for
its contribution to the youth service in London. Yet it would be churlish not to
acknowledge the steady support Devas has received over the years. The policy
of partnership between the voluntary and statutory sectors, though not without
its moments of frisson, has worked well and successive youth officers have made*

valuable contributions to Council discussions and in support to the seconded
workers at the club. Management and staff have grown accustomed to the
Authority's guidance and protection. Devas would not be as it is today were it
not for the ILEA."

The Federation was deeply concerned, however, that the transfer of responsibilities from the ILEA to the inner London Boroughs would put at risk the grant-aid to its headquarters operation and its London–wide servicing of clubs and the funding of paid club leaders, both full–time and part–time. At the point of transfer, which took effect in April 1990, there was no clarification from the Government of what resources would be allocated to the Boroughs. To avert this crisis, the Federation prepared a detailed application to the Department of Education and Science for funds to support its work. The application was successful, and the ILEA grant of £100,000 was replaced by funding from the Department of Education and Science, limited to a yearly application over a three year period, and from the London Borough Grants Committee. It obtained funding from charitable sources to establish two posts which would be responsible for liaising with the new London local education authorities and supporting those clubs which were particularly at risk.

The funding uncertainties were exacerbated by the increasing pressures on charities. Trusts, livery companies and other donors which had traditionally supported the Fed were now facing claims from many other organisations. The prime example of this shift was the City Parochial Foundation, which in 1988–89 decided not to renew its long–standing grant, first given in 1926, because it wanted to spread its support to other worthy causes.

In these turbulent times, the Federation was buoyed up in 1988–89 by the publication of an HMI report on the NABC and a number of its constituent organisations. The Fed was found to be 'well managed and its clubs well resourced, backed up with a clear sense of purpose and commitment'. Its capacity to cope with set–backs was demonstrated in the way it responded to the damage and chaos caused at Hindleap by the great storm of 16 October 1988:

> *"Whilst there was only minor damage to the buildings, the forest was for the*
> *most part unrecognisable, with access to the centre completely blocked and all*
> *16 miles of forest tracks impassable. By noon of the first day, staff had cleared*
> *122 fallen trees. For the next two weeks, they had cut through to the main A22*
> *road; repaired high and low ropes; rebuilt the obstacle courses; constructed*
> *a new abseil platform; made safe hundreds of partly fallen trees and cleared*
> *approximately six miles of forest ride."*

Less havoc was caused at Woodrow High House, but the support of local volunteers enabled the damage to be quickly cleared, demonstrating the strength of the partnership between the centre and the local community.

The drive to extend and improve the Fed's facilities continued, as a major refurbishment programme was commenced at Woodrow High House at this time, made possible by the generosity of the Joseph Levy Charitable Foundation and the Variety Club of Great Britain. The bedrooms were improved and toilets for the disabled were added.

In 1989, as a response to the new administrative arrangements in local government, the Federation set up a special Review Committee to examine its servicing and developmental role in anticipation of the difficulties that clubs would encounter in the wake of the ILEA's demise. A new Development Services team was created, and four officers assumed the responsibility for supporting and developing all aspects of club work. It was thought that this team would provide a more concentrated and comprehensive service to all affiliated clubs.

Though the Fed was safeguarded in the short term by transitional grants, it was unimpressed by the ability of the London Boroughs to rise to the challenge of taking over the ILEA's responsibilities, as the 1990–91 annual report complained:

> "We were told by senior politicians 'not to worry' only to be rewarded by a proliferation of separate educational bureaucracies, each with its own philosophy. All this may appear to be retrospective carping, but put simply our clubs are struggling for survival and, as with the poll tax, the time for urgent evaluation is now. It is our view that the inner London Boroughs do not have the resources to develop effectively their statutory obligations, whilst equally supporting a proper commitment to the voluntary sector. As a result, voluntary groups and organisations, whose dedication and work for over a century has been the bedrock of any stable and civilised society, are now seriously at risk. We therefore urge Her Majesty's Government to review the current state of the Youth Service across the London area following the replacement of a unified education authority by a disparate group of local education authorities."

Notwithstanding its criticism of the devolution of powers to the twelve Boroughs, the Fed sought to develop close links with them:

> "All these offer opportunities for a more locally based and, therefore, responsive voluntary youth sector, but only if there is full consultation and co-operation between the voluntary youth services and the statutory sector."

To facilitate such consultation and co-operation, Club Services Officers liaised closely with the Youth Officers in the Boroughs on matters of policy, finance and club development. They also spent a considerable amount of time in advising and supporting member clubs and staff through this difficult process of devolution.

Yet, having survived the immediate point of transition, the Federation was soon addressing the unresolved issue of continued funding from the Department of Education and Science, as the annual report for 1990–91 highlighted:

> "We are greatly concerned that no arrangements have been made to replace the (DES) funding after that date (March 1993). At club level, there have been some dramatic reductions in grants from borough councils, and this has increased the pressure on resources made available to clubs by the Fed."

A new scheme of funding was finally agreed, though again with a guarantee for only three years. However, this gave the Federation a valuable breathing space, though it was forced in 1993 to sell some of its long-term investments to maintain liquidity.

This was also a period of serious debate about youth work issues. The Federation had felt increasingly under pressure to re-examine its focus on working with boys. In 1988, it had reiterated that this focus remained relevant:

"We remain firmly committed to the view that our work with boys and young men is entirely relevant and that given sufficient resources we can continue to make a distinctive contribution in this important area of work…The intensity of political pressure has been such that the Federation decided to adopt a more positive stance by publishing a document, 'Profile and Background'. This document set out to restate our current position, giving due consideration and weight to emerging areas of work which included youth unemployment, racism, young people and drugs, young people and the police and anti-sexist youth work.

The Fed and its member clubs have experienced and will continue to experience attacks which stem either from a lack of information or from a deliberate attempt to undermine our work, by those who seek to deny young people the right to choose how and where they wish to spend their leisure time."

In 1993, however, the Fed set up a strategic review to respond to the NABC's decision to extend membership to girls and young women. The Fed had seen the 1990 HMI report, which had emphasised the importance of its role of developing boys' work through the boys' club movement, as a formal endorsement of the value of separate provision for boys and young men, encouraging it to withstand any external pressures to alter its traditional stance on this issue. Yet the NABC's changing attitude, and the fact that many clubs were now admitting girls and young women as a regular feature of club life, caused the Federation to reconsider its formal position. After much discussion and reflection, presided over with tact by Neil Maitland as Chair (the club with which he had a long association was the Crown and Manor), an Emergency General Meeting voted on 17 June 1994 by a large majority to admit girls and young women into membership and to change the organisation's name to the London Federation of Clubs for Young People, to take effect from 1 September 1994. This change was welcomed by the vast majority of the Federation's membership, as is demonstrated by these reflections in the 1993–94 annual report of the Devas Club:

"One further change that has taken place in the course of the year gives cause for unqualified rejoicing. The LFBC has voted overwhelmingly to amend its rules and other instruments so that its services shall, in future, be available equally to females as well as males. From 1st September, the name changes to the London Federation of Clubs for Young People. In practice, the differences may be almost imperceptible. But as far as Devas is concerned, the psychological advantage of having the rules in line with current practice is considerable. We applaud the Fed Chairman, Neil Maitland, on his patience and diplomacy in bringing this about."

This momentous change prompted an immediate revision in the organisation's statement of objectives to bring it in line with the newly agreed and broadened focus:

"The Fed's main objective is to give young people access to a range of learning opportunities and challenging experiences which promote their personal and social development."

This opening up of full membership to girls and young women was also matched by a declaration that equality of opportunity extended to other special and often marginalized groups: 'to ensure that young people have equality of opportunity to make use of the available resources and services of the Federation, regardless of age, race, religion, national origin, marital status, disability or sexual orientation'. To avoid any blurring of its identity that this new receptiveness might suggest, the Fed still felt the need to assert its separateness as a youth organisation and to emphasise that there remained a distinctive role for specialist provision for boys and young men:

"The Fed remains a separate organisation, which would be equally accessible to both sexes, whilst continuing to affirm specialist work with boys and young men and encouraging specialist work with girls and young women."

With the appointment of Noel Vallely as Chief Executive in January 1995, the Federation accelerated its efforts to intensify its grappling with contemporary youth work issues. Noel Vallely had been Assistant National Secretary of the National Council of the YMCA, and brought experience of youth work training and organisational change to the Fed. Staff developed approaches to the topical concerns of racism, sexism, drug abuse, crime and other social issues which affected the lives of young people. Crime Action Groups were developed in clubs as a practical response by club members to petty crime, bullying and vandalism. Any lingering doubts about the relevance of 'community' approaches associated with the Milson–Fairbairn Report were dispersed by the Fed's involvement in an Estates Project funded by the Department for Education and the Vivien Duffield Foundation. This project–located on housing estates within the reach of Fed clubs in Brixton, Poplar, Lewisham, Regents Park, Southwark and Waltham Forest–aimed to bring about a greater degree of community involvement in youth work provision. The Fed also joined in a project called 'Roadrunners' in association with the NABC–CYP, Crime Concern and Sun Alliance. The project was designed to increase young people's awareness of issues around driving: practical driving skills, the finances of driving and purchasing a second–hand car. It was hoped that this kind of project would attract the older 15–17 year age group, who were becoming less visible in the ranks of club members. The organisation also worked with Mencap and the London Union of Youth Clubs on The Access Project, which integrated young people with learning disabilities into mainstream youth clubs. The ability of all clubs to respond to these new emphases was facilitated by the encouragement and support offered by Club Services Officers, whose pivotal role was praised in 1997 by one of Her Majesty's Inspectors:

"The level of visiting currently undertaken by the team is exceptionally frequent. Collectively they have a picture of club–based youth work in London no other team can match."

It was not unusual for an officer to visit clubs on every weekday evening and then attend a sporting competition or a residential conference at the weekend. This level of intense commitment was epitomised by Peter Hunter, who was employed at the Fed from 1974 to 2007 in a number of capacities, including Club Services Officer, with a brief for outdoor pursuits, Senior Club Services Officer and Assistant General Secretary. His unstinting dedication and his ready helpfulness to club leaders and management committees were outstanding. Throughout his time with the organisation, he was a source of instant and dependable information and guidance on all matters relating to London Youth. The constancy as well as the frequency of this quality and level of support was complimented by Lenny Elms of the Poplar Boys' and Girls' Club:

> *"We value extremely highly the support given by the Fed which has resulted in recruitment for the club management committee, liaison support with the local authority and grants towards the refurbishment of the club."*

The Federation's move towards a more inclusive youth work agenda, and increasing involvement in joint work with other organisations, created the conditions in which it could give more serious consideration to the benefits of forging a closer relationship with the London Union of Youth Clubs.

Awards ceremony, 1997

The London Union of Youth Clubs and its Antecedents

The antecedents of the London Union of Youth Clubs follow a parallel pattern to that of the London Federation. Indeed, its roots go back even further to 1880. This was the year in which the Girls' Club Union was formed in order to foster closer links between girls' clubs. Much of the inspiration and drive for this development came from Maude Stanley. She founded the Soho Club for Girls in 1880. It was originally set up in Porter Street, but moved to new premises in Greek Street in 1883. A wall plaque now marks its origins:

"59 Greek Street was built in 1883 as the Soho Club and Home for Working Girls. In the 1920s it became the Theatre Girls' Club, a home for women working in the theatre and later a hostel for homeless women."

Even before she set up the Soho Club for Girls, Maude Stanley had worked with boys in the Five Dials area, just off the Charing Cross Road and St Martin's Lane in central London:

"About five years ago I determined to try what I could do with these poor boys, who from their very civility to myself I felt were open to the refining influence of a woman's teaching. So in February 1873, after knowing the neighbourhood for three years, I began a School on Sunday afternoons. I invited four boys to come, these brought others, and from that time to August, I had a varying number of from eight to twenty–five every Sunday. I began the School with a working shoemaker, who lived in the next street, and later I had a postman to help; but he was always called 'Squint Eye' by the boys, from a personal defect and he never got much hold over them. The shoemaker's temper and patience used to be sorely tried: as for mine, I felt it no trial, for the fact of contending with the determined mischief of some of the boys, had in it the delight of a fight, in which I was generally victorious…

The moment of trial was the end of the school. As long as I could keep the boys under my eye, they were tolerably well behaved, and to call them by name was generally sufficient to restore order; but if, when the prayer was finished, my attention was wanted at the door, and I could no longer keep watch over the ladder, down they would rush, and make hideous confusion with the faggots,– and one day lighted a match and narrowly escaped burning down the house."
('Work About the Five Dials', Maude Stanley, 1878.)

Her main focus, however, was on developing clubs for girls. In 1876, she established a Girls' Night School in the same premises where the boys met. The school was initially open on three nights a week, but a decline in numbers led quickly to its closure. In its place, Stanley began a weekly sewing class:

"It is for those who have left school and are at work in trades or at home. They readily bring their pennies to pay for the class, and we teach them needlework and cutting out, and great is the delight of these poor girls to be able to go home and show their mothers that they can cut out a shift. The best of mothers could

Maude Stanley

not well teach their girls to cut out in one crowded room which is occupied by the whole family day and night; and nothing contributes more to the comfort of the home of a working man than when his wife can make his shifts and the children's clothes, instead of buying them ready–made, as many do in London, a cheap article perhaps, but ill–sewn and a poor material." ('Work About the Five Dials', Maude Stanley, 1878.)

It is clear from this extract that the activities at the centre of a girls' club were related to domestic skills, rather than the competitive sports on offer at the boys' clubs of the time:

"The nature of much girls' club work at that time tended to place an emphasis on relationships and gentle improvement, so that girls may 'ennoble the class to which they belong' (Stanley). This could be contrasted with the talk of character–building and muscular Christianity that could be found around

boys' work." ('Maude Stanley, girls' clubs and district visiting', reproduced from the encyclopaedia of informal education, 2012.)

Lily Montagu was another early pioneer of girls' clubs. In 1893, supported by her younger sister, Marian, she founded the West Central Jewish Girls' Club in the back streets off Oxford Street, providing evening classes in various subjects for working girls. These classes included language, literature and culture, music appreciation, opera, drama, needlework, handicrafts, psychology, citizenship, photography, dancing, dressmaking, cooking and millinery. In pursuing this work, Lily Montagu had to struggle against the prejudices of the time and the misgivings of her parents, as she revealed in her book, 'My Club and I':

> *"For myself, I had at the beginning of my Club career the sympathetic encouragement of my parents. They were convinced that it was desirable and altogether right and proper for young girls to have some outlet in social service. It was only when the small beginning grew until it absorbed my life, and made me give practically whole time service, that I came up against parental anxiety and concern.*
>
> *The accepted life's programme for every girl in my set was that she should go out as much as possible, know plenty of 'nice people' and settle down at an early age in marriage. My complete failure to conform with this widely supported plan brought much disappointment and anxiety to those who loved me, and the ladies of my mother's visiting circle, though generally kind and sympathetic, did not approve of my mode of life and outlook. Because I worked very hard, dressed badly, went out very little, was always shy and awkward at social functions, I was held up as a warning by mother's acquaintances...(and they) kept their daughters away from my bad influence."* ('My Club and I', Lily Montagu, 1943.)

Her shyness and awkwardness disappeared, however, when she supervised the activities of the club. She insisted that her approach to the girls was based on 'just friendliness'. This simple tenet helped to create a 'spirit' within the club, which she depicted in these terms:

> *"An inherent spirit of decency, obedience, friendship and comradeship, and of absolute loyalty, is present everywhere. The young people behave freely and without inhibitions. They enjoy themselves loudly and exhibit no shyness or undue modesty. Yet a kind of natural restraint, born from the indefinable spirit which is characteristic of the Club, always keeps them in the right hands. It is obvious that they enjoy not only the social and educational amenities of the Club, but that they find in it a spiritual outlet for all their better tendencies. They are happy at the Club and come regularly because of the 'simple friendship' which is given them by one whose generosity in imparting it is unbounded."*

Though Lily Montagu ceased to attend the club on a regular basis as her other activities at national and international level increased, she continued to visit the club on one evening each week and on Sundays throughout her life.

In later decades, the Girls' Club Union launched in 1880 by Maude Stanley and others underwent a series of mergers. It became known later as the London Girls' Club Union; and in the late 1930s it amalgamated with the Federation of Girls' Clubs (linked to the Young Women's Christian Association) and the Social Institutes' Union to form the London Union of Girls' Clubs. Throughout all of these changes and mergers, the organisation preserved its focus on girls' clubs. At a national level, Lily Montagu was a prime mover behind the formation in 1911 of the National Organisation of Girls' Clubs. (This body was succeeded in 1926 by the National Association of Girls' Clubs.) She chaired the NOGC for many years and later became its co–President.

Though there was little active dialogue and joint activity between the National Organisation and the organisations that represented boys' clubs during these years, Lily Montagu's letters reveal that she developed close relationships at a personal level with prominent supporters of the London Federation of Boys' Clubs. She knew Basil Henriques through their involvement in the West London and Liberal Jewish Synagogue. Henriques ran the Oxford and St George's Club in Berner Street in Whitechapel, and was prominent in the affairs of both the National Association of Boys' Clubs and the London Federation of Boys' Clubs. He acknowledged his debt to Lily Montagu in a letter to her written on 19 September 1952:

> *"From the time when I came down from Oxford you have had a very great influence over me, and no words can adequately express my gratitude to you."*

She was approached in November 1923 by W.McG. Eagar (the author of 'Making Men', a former warden of the Oxford and Bermondsey Club and a leading advocate of the case for a national association to represent boys' clubs) to join the Board of Directors of the newly formed National Public Utility Society. Eagar was at this time the Secretary of The Garden Cities and Town Planning Association, which wanted to set up the new organisation to provide improved housing conditions for people who lived in overcrowded conditions.

During the Second World War, the London Union sought to continue its activities in as undisturbed way as possible. The blitz disrupted the life of clubs in the first years of the war, and some clubs lost their premises amid the devastation of the air raids. One of those clubs was the West Central Club. On 17 April 1941, bombing destroyed the club building, killing 27 people and destroying all the organisation's records and archives. Lily Montagu wrote a club letter to members in May after the destruction of the building, with these words of exhortation and encouragement:

> *"Our Club gave us fine opportunities to cultivate friendship. It was a democracy in which each individual counted and was given affection and encouragement to realise as fully as possible the powers of her or his personality. The Club asks each one of us to give the best service we could to the welfare of the whole. Above all, we were offered a conception of a living Judaism, and were expected to express our religion as fully as possible in our lives. The friends who have been taken from us shared these Club ideals, and in honouring their memory I ask you to be more zealous in your loyalty."*

The Union's headquarters in Clapham was also the casualty of a bomb in the blitz, resulting in the loss of the organisation's archives and records. This loss explains why it is possible to give only a sketchy account of its history between its early days and 1942.

In 1942, 200 clubs were affiliated members, with 1,000 girls in membership. The Union worked closely with the LCC to ensure that classes continued to be offered. In a scheme to provide free demonstration classes, 18 clubs were chosen to accommodate a number of classes, the most popular of which were Greek and dancing, clay modelling, toy making, music appreciation, vocal music and brains trusts. In 1943, the Union held a conference on anti–semitism and fascism. It also showed its support for the victims of fascism by promoting an appeal by the Polish Children's Rescue Fund, which raised funds for Polish children evacuated to Persia. It also expressed its disappointment to the Government about its unwillingness to release people from civil defence duties to run junior clubs. Examples were given of volunteers who had been running clubs, only to give it up because their civil defence duties were too onerous and tiring. The Union's Executive Committee registered its strong feeling that 'youth leadership was as good a contribution to National Service as voluntary work on civil defence'. The request of Mrs Collingwood, the Union's Assistant Organising Secretary, for compassionate leave in April 1944, is a reminder of the impact of the war conditions on everyday life:

> *"Mrs Collingwood's little daughter was very nervous of air raids–Mrs Collingwood has asked whether she might have three weeks' holiday immediately in order to accompany her daughter into a safe area."*

In the same year, the Union pressed for the provision of huts to accommodate clubs, which had lost their premises due to bomb damage in South London and elsewhere. It argued that priority in obtaining alternative accommodation should be given to those clubs which had lost their premises and informed those clubs which were affected of the British War Relief Society's grants for equipment. The person who was responsible for holding the organisation together during the war years was Miss Ross, who retired as its Organising Secretary in April 1944. She was particularly thanked for her 'splendid pioneer work' in bringing eleven different organisations into the new framework of the London Union of Girls' Clubs.

A sign of co–operation between the London Union and the London Federation of Boys' Clubs was the establishment in April 1942 of the London Association of Mixed Clubs, a joint section to foster mixed clubs as a complementary development to the existing girls' clubs and boys' clubs. Sir Charles Wrench of the London Federation gave the new organisation a loan of £20 to open an account, so that initial expenses could be met at once. Affiliation fees soon reached £40. The expansion of mixed clubs, and the co–operation between the two London–wide organisations, prompted suggestions for a more permanent unified approach. In January 1945, the Union's Executive Committee discussed the possibility of reconstituting itself as the London Union of Girls' Clubs and Mixed Clubs after consultation with the London Association of Mixed Clubs. It offered the London Federation adequate representation on any newly constituted body. A youth leaders' meeting in May 1945 submitted this statement to the Union and the Federation:

> *"This conference believes that youth work in London can best be done under one organisation catering for Girls', Boys' and Mixed Work. It further recommends that the national bodies should give this matter their attention."*

In April 1946, the Union's Council agreed that it should support mixed clubs as well as girls' clubs and girls in mixed clubs. To reflect this policy shift, the organisation changed its name to the London Union of Mixed Clubs and Girls' Clubs. Interestingly, similar discussions had taken place at national level, though the National Association of Girls' Clubs decided that it should in future be called the National Association of Girls' Clubs and Mixed Clubs. It is unclear whether the different ordering of the nomenclature revealed any real difference in emphasis or approach! In January 1944, the National Association had debated three possible names–the National Association of Girls' Clubs and Mixed Clubs; the National Association of Youth Clubs (Girls' and Mixed); and an entirely new name yet to be decided. Though the second option was strongly opposed by the National Association of Boys' Clubs, it was eventually to become the revised name of the organisation. The Union's Executive Committee had played its part in the debate by urging the national body to devise a name which 'would be more inspiring, original and modern to get away from the word Association or Union'. Its own suggestion was Youth Clubs of England or Youth Clubs of Britain not adopted at the time, but to have an application at a subsequent date!

Despite the incorporation of mixed clubs, the Union still maintained its primary focus on girls' work and the assertion of their interests. It was vehement in its criticism of a London Youth Committee conference held in 1944, on the grounds that girls' work was largely ignored and that there was no woman represented on the platform. In the immediate post–war years (when Margaret Bondfield, who had become the first ever woman Cabinet minister when she was appointed Minister of Labour by Ramsay MacDonald in June 1929, was President), the organisation concentrated on securing its future and increasing its profile. In November 1946, a policy group discussed two possible directions for the Union's work: one as an active, affiliating body, visiting and providing services to the increasing number of clubs in the area; and the alternative as a focus of specialism in club techniques, advising the statutory authorities on training and related areas of work. The reality was that the first option was the main direction in which the Union steered. In July 1946, it sought to protect the interests of its affiliated groups in this recommendation to the LCC:

> "The LCC be urged to make the main average, nightly attendance required as a condition of grant aid towards a leader's salary considerably lower than 60, and that attention should be drawn to the importance of appointing men and women in mixed clubs. It is also suggested that more than one leader will normally be necessary if junior work were to be done as well as senior within the club."

In 1947, activities such as football, netball, drama, music and ballroom dancing constituted the core of the centrally organised programme. Club members also participated in adventurous holidays to France, Germany, Holland, Italy and Spain.

But this main preoccupation did not prevent the Union from completely disregarding its potential role as a group of specialists in club techniques. In July 1947, it linked up with the Heads of LCC evening institutes for a conference on 'Informal Education', designed to induct instructors in the overall purpose and methods of club work.

In consolidating its position, the Union was faced by financial problems. In May 1949, the Treasurer pointed out that, unless new money was raised, the Union would not be solvent at the end of the year. It did remain solvent, largely due to a gift of £500 from the Goldsmiths' Company and receipts from charity shows performed by Joyce Grenfell (the actress and comedienne and a Vice–President of the Union). In these circumstances of stringency–a sign of its continuing priorities–the Union decided that it had no money at its disposal to give grant aid to boys in mixed clubs.

In the 1950s and 1960s, the Union was reporting on a considerable extension of its work with clubs and members. There was an increase in the number of the organisation's Field Officers to cope with this expansion. The Union expanded from 280 clubs in 1968 to 700 in 1973 with no further increase in its complement of staff, making it a struggle to visit clubs on a regular basis.

In the 1970s, the Union began to develop its reputation of responding in innovative ways to contemporary issues. In 1977, at a time of national concern about the increasing levels of youth employment, it submitted proposals to the Manpower Services Commission to develop a scheme, which would take on 60 unemployed young people as assistants to full-time youth leaders. In the previous year, the Union had attempted to stay in the vanguard of ground-breaking and project – based youth work practice by setting up the Community Education Project. Schemes were initiated in clubs to give members an understanding of how society was organised, how decisions were made and how they could influence them.

The Union continued to operate in a testing financial climate. It marked its centenary in 1980 by mounting an ambitious public appeal for funds 'in order that the London Union might survive into the 80s'. The target of the appeal was £100,000, and income had reached £40,800 by 1981. The Union raised £229,000 from the sale of 59 Greek Street (the base of Maude Stanley's work with girls).

The shape of the Union's work in the 1980s was illustrated by the nature of the panels set up to oversee its work: girls' work, employment, arts and drama, sports and competitions, training and outdoor pursuits. Yet much discussion centred on the dilemma of sustaining these developments in times of economic stringency and the resultant need to reduce the deficit to manageable proportions. The Union argued the case that new grants should include the full cost of administrative overheads. In 1982, the conditions for full membership were these: each club/group should have a minimum of 12 in membership; two-thirds of members should be between 11 and 21 years of age; members should meet regularly, at least once a week; and members should be encouraged to participate and share in the responsibilities of manageme nt.

The Union received the Thompson Report on the Youth Service with a positive if cautious welcome:

> *"In general, we welcome the review and support its recommendations. But we would not wish to give the report an unqualified welcome; we feel the report is not specific enough in some areas, and is not sufficiently far–reaching in others."*

It offered a number of suggestions to add specificity and vision to the report's recommendations. It thought that the improved links between young people and the police should be highlighted; that greater emphasis should be put on the contribution of the Youth Service to social education; that unemployed young people should be offered further opportunities after they had come to the end of the Youth Training scheme; and that the Youth

Service should be given additional resources to 'meet the challenges that society is placing upon it', such as unemployment, racism and crime.

The Union took some pride in its reputation as a pioneer. In 1984, it claimed to be the only local association within the National Association of Youth Clubs, which placed a specific emphasis on work with girls and young women. Its work on race equality was deemed to be 'the only project of its sort'. The Union was certainly in the forefront of efforts within the Youth Service to set youth work within a broader equal opportunities framework. It was prominent in the moves during this time to ensure that young people with mobility problems were not excluded from buildings.

Nevertheless, the Union in the early 1980s continued to stress the centrality of girls' work to its agenda. It spelled out in 1984 what it meant by its distinctive approach to this area of work:

> *"Girls' work refers to work being carried out by women youth workers to encourage the full participation and potential of young women, to increase the range of choices available to young women, and to give them confidence to use these choices, and to encourage attitudes against sexist and racist stereotyping. Girls' work does not mean merely girls' nights or girls' groups, but a new approach."*

An indication of this new approach was the work plan formulated by the Girls' Work Unit. Ten activity boxes, containing materials for particular pursuits, such as carpentry, enamelling and jewellery, were prepared for use in clubs. They were intended to 'help women in clubs to involve girls in clubs which still often centre around the eternal pool table'.

The funding of girls' work was supported by the establishment of the London Girls' Fund in 1985. The Fund brought together a number of trusts of which the London Union was the trustee, including the Maude Stanley Working Girls' Club Fund, the Maude Stanley Fund for Working Girls' Clubs and Holiday Homes, the Soho Working Girls' Clubs, the Rachel Mansfield Memorial Trust, and the Clifton House and Gilbert Bartholomew Memorial Fund. The declared purpose of the new Fund was 'to promote the welfare of girls in London by providing for them facilities in youth clubs and youth groups in London and holidays'. In 1986, it was decided that the annual income from the London Girls' Fund should be used to benefit girls and young women. In 1986–87, £10,300 was made available in this way: £2,800 as small grants for girls' work; £1,000 for girls' only activities and training for women youth workers; £3,000 for a girls' work consultant to support clubs in additional Boroughs; and £3,500 for a worker to develop resources for work with girls and young women.

The Union continued to take a lead in responding to the growing problem of youth unemployment. It became involved in the Community Enterprise programme in 1979. Of the 104 unemployed young people who completed the programme in 1982, 19 obtained a full–time college place to undertake a qualifying course in youth and community work; 11 obtained full–time jobs at an agency where they had a placement; 25 obtained employment elsewhere; and 12 took up part–time work. The work on this front expanded to such an extent that by 1985 the Union was employing 23 full–time staff and 230 part–time workers. Young people on the various schemes were offered a variety of work and training opportunities in agencies which worked with children, young people, the elderly and adults with disabilities. The organisation's success in setting up schemes to tackle youth unemployment led it in 1985 to set up London Employment Training

Youth workers at The Working with Young Women through the 90s Conference

as a company with its own memoranda and articles of association. Its object was 'to advance the education and training of underprivileged and needy people by providing them or assisting in providing them with vocational training work skills and work experience'.

The Union heralded in the 1990s with the publication of a Ten Year Plan. The main aim was 'to assist and improve youth work which encourages the personal and social development of young people in clubs and groups in London, and particularly those in priority areas or groups such as girls and young women'. The re–articulated objectives sought to build on the traditional strengths of the Union and to adapt the 1974 constitution to a new concern for project–based, experimental and 'model' work within a clear equal opportunities framework:

> *"– to provide effective support for clubs and groups in membership*
>
> *– to carry out model work with young people through activities, projects, training, and youth advocacy, ensuring that there is participation by young people in this work and in LUYC*
>
> *– to deliver work through an educational curriculum which has an equal opportunities framework on priority areas and groups, including small/isolated clubs and LUYC's historical commitment to work with girls and young women."*

But this renewal of purpose was instantly buffeted by new financial storms. Simon Abbott, the Union's Chief Executive appointed in 1982, reported in 1989:

> "LUYC has for long been under stress, from attempting to do too much, from attempting to service many clubs, from having inadequate funding, particularly for the 'core' (i.e. office and management servicing). Increased uncertainty over future funding and patterns of work has added to the stress and frustration."

The immediate uncertainty over funding was caused by the abolition of the ILEA in 1990. In 1989–90, the Union was faced by an overall deficit of £66,000 and doubts about whether the ILEA grant would be replaced. Finally, it was decided that, for the 1990–91 financial year, the organisation would receive £41,175 from the Department for Education and Science and £50,360 from the London Boroughs Grants Unit. This settlement was intended to last for three years, but uncertainty persisted about the years beyond 1993. The Union's case was taken up by Lord Dormand of Easington in the House of Lords on 19 December 1989 in a question to the Minister, Viscount Davidson:

> "Can he say what will happen to the headquarters of the various voluntary youth organisations when the Government grant comes to an end in 1993? I ask that because I understand that there is an interim Government grant effective from 1990 to 1993. Does not the noble Viscount agree that such bodies as the London Union of Youth Clubs, the LFBC, the boy scouts, the girl guides and the Woodcraft Folk, and so on, perform a vital function in the London youth service?"

In his response, Viscount Davidson spelled out the arrangements for the interim funding and emphasised that the umbrella organisations, which were receiving the money, had not expressed any dissatisfaction with the amount. This insistence provoked a strong response from the Union's Chair, Sonia Palmer, in a letter to Viscount Davidson on 18 January 1990:

> "Under the DES special grants programme, we have been offered less than half (almost 46%) of our current year's ILEA funding which would almost certainly have continued next year with some allowance for inflation had ILEA itself continued. We are in effect 'losing' about £65,000. The situation therefore is that we have not expressed dissatisfaction to the DES, because we do value the grants offered (and because we have been firmly advised that no more is on offer from the DES). But we are deeply dismayed at the disastrous financial situation we shall shortly enter, under which our services for 500 clubs must be reduced."

The main developments of the 1990s were the moves towards a possible merger with the Association of Combined Youth Clubs (an organisation based mainly in South London with 120 clubs in membership) and the London Federation. In 1984, there had been a proposal that there should be closer co–operation between the Union and the Federation. This did lead to the attendance of Neil Maitland, the Federation's then Chair, at Union committee meetings as an observer in 1985 and to a joint tackling of such shared problems as rate capping and the abolition of the ILEA, but it did not result in any firm and decisive steps towards a unified organisation in London. Discussions between the national bodies (Youth Clubs UK, as the NAYC had now become, and the National Association of Boys' Clubs) in 1991, and hints that the new principal funders (the Department for Education and Science and the London Borough Grants Unit) would look with favour on increased collaboration or even amalgamation, put the issue back on the agenda.

A joint meeting was held between the Chief Executives of LUYC, LFBC and the Association of Combined Youth Clubs (ACYC). They expressed a concern that any pressure from the statutory funders should not be allowed to affect the independence of each organization, but a joint statement confirmed that there was a desire to continue the explorations:

> *"We thought that there was advantage in spelling out in brief terms our specialist areas and that there might be the opportunities for some joint working around training."*

Further discussions in July 1991 between the officers of the Union and the Federation, however, revealed that there was no wish to go beyond collaborative work. It was agreed that, well short of amalgamation, there should be further exchange on curriculum and services; a shared activities event; joint lobbying; and a continuing dialogue.

Negotiations with the ACYC got off the ground more quickly and seriously than with the Federation. Two meetings were held in 1992 to determine what the prospects were for closer co–operation. In May 1992, CERT (the Charities Effectiveness Review Trust) was commissioned to carry out a consultancy on the prospects at a cost of £8,500. The report of the consultants (Jill Pitkeathley, then Director of the National Carers' Association and later the Chair of the New Opportunities Fund, one of the lottery distributors, and Michael Butterfield, the General Secretary of the National Association of Youth Clubs from 1975 to 1986) recommended that merger should go ahead. Initially, the discussions were positive, focusing on aligning the ACYC's strengths in junior work and activities with the LUYC's focus on the older age group and issue–based youth work. However, discussions faltered in 1994, when the ACYC decided that it could not adhere to the previously agreed timetable for merger in 1995. The Chair of the LUYC asked the ACYC's Chair to identify any areas of the Union's current work that was unclear or causing concern to the ACYC. A letter of 8 June 1994 from Sir Michael Harrison, the Chair of ACYC and a Lloyd's insurance broker, revealed ACYC's misgivings about merger:

> *"It is clear that there remains a substantial concern about the situation and development of face–to–face work with children and young people and the support of small voluntary units. This is, as you know, the traditional approach which ACYC has maintained over the past thirty plus years, and also the area which needs to be absorbed within the whole work of the new organisation. There is therefore in all our discussions a feeling that the work with a younger age range, and the development of a programme of events and competitions, will be a second priority."*

This exchange effectively ended the moves towards amalgamation, and in March 1995 ACYC formally stated that it did not wish to join the LUYC in a new youth organisation in London, though there was a continuing dialogue for a while about partnership working (subsequently, in 1999, the ACYC changed its name to Young People @ Now).

The Union maintained its interest in some form of unification in London, and gave some attention to what a 'new organisation' would look like. The consultants, though their brief had been to make recommendations on the organisational coming together of the LUYC and the ACYC, had given a broad intimation that a more realistic and effective scenario for the future was a search for common ground between the LUYC and the LFBC:

> "On the face of it there is little to encourage the London Federation to join up with anyone else. However, times are changing, and it could well be that the hon. officers and officials in the London Federation of Boys' Clubs might recognize the importance of a unified body for club work in London working for boys, girls and boys and girls together."

This intimation clearly influenced the Union in its reflections on the prospects for the future, as this extract from the 1994 paper, "Developing the 'New Organisation'" shows:

> "We also know that the changes at what is now the London Federation of Clubs for Young People (they now include girls in their work and will have a new Chief Executive) are in many ways more important for LUYC than what happens in any other youth organisation. This is because the Fed has substantial resources and loyalties on the youth club scene in London."

Up to the eventual point of amalgamation with the London Federation in 1999, the Union continued to build on its strengths to develop new projects. Its development plan in 1993 attempted to sharpen the organisation's focus:

> "The main aim is to assist and improve youth work which encourages the personal and social development of young people in clubs and groups in London, and particularly those in priority areas or groups such as girls and young women."

The plan set out the Union's intention to target its work more selectively on these areas of work: isolated/small clubs; inner city estates; young black and Asian people; young gay and lesbian people; young people with disabilities; and girls and young women.

The Union's receptiveness to new opportunities is demonstrated by its aspiration, articulated in December 1994, to develop a European dimension to its work:

> "LUYC is committed to developing a strategic role within European youth work structures. It is committed to actively participating in European youth work initiatives, networks, structures and activities which will expressly benefit young people and those working with them."

As a result of this new policy, a number of youth exchanges took place to and from European countries, and young people took part in a major conference in France to develop European strategies in relation to shared youth work issues.

Other initiatives which demonstrated the Union's commitment to innovative projects included: Young Women into Safer Surroundings; Quality Youth Work (the Department for Education and Employment gave funding to promote a quality approach to youth work); the Inclusion Project (a joint project with Mencap and the London Federation of Clubs for Young People to ensure that young people with learning difficulties could gain access to 'mainstream' youth provision); and the London Young People's Environmental Network. In late 1996, the Lotteries Charity Board gave a grant of £30,000 per annum for three years to the Union to cover the costs of a Fieldwork Director, a half–time Youth Achievements Awards post (the Awards represented a pioneering, peer–led and assessed means of recognising young people's non–academic achievements), and related operating and overheads costs.

Members of London Environmental Young People's Network showing off their magazine N-GAGE

A new project, 'Youth Sport', was developed jointly with the London Federation of Clubs for Young People and the Middlesex Young People's Clubs. The Sports Council granted £27,000 per year for three years from November 1995 to enable the three partners to provide sports training and sports development to young people, youth clubs and youth groups. A sign of the increasing co–operation and understanding between the Union and the Federation was the agreement that the Union would be the employer, and the Federation the supervisor, of the project officer.

The positive outcomes of collaborative projects of this kind created a climate in which amalgamation with the LFCYP became a more feasible proposition. The Sir John Cass Foundation had also at this time brought a number of youth organisations together to debate the need for a single London–wide youth organisation. Though this particular intervention came to nothing, it constituted another contributing factor in the changing climate. A new management team (Mark Wakefield, a member of the Union's Management Committee and Borough Youth Officer in Newham, became Chief Executive in 1996, and Sir David Knox, who had retired as MP for Staffordshire Moorlands at the 1997 general election, became Chair of the Management Committee in that year) saw the inevitability, and grasped the potential, of a unified organisation for youth work in the capital. A survey of members, as part of a review of LUYC's role and purpose, also confirmed that over 90% of them would like to see a single organisation representing youth work in London. Sir David Knox, in his introduction to the Union's final annual review of December 1998, declared his commitment to amalgamation in ambitious terms:

> *"We intend that the new organisation will provide better support and services for the members of both bodies than we have previously offered separately and that it will seek to raise the profile and importance of youth work provision in London. I believe that this is the most radical and exciting development in the youth work sector in the Capital for several generations with tremendous potential and we must all work to ensure that it is successful."*

6. The Era of Integration, 1999–2013

The budget cuts of the Thatcher and Major years continued to inhibit the development of the Youth Service in the New Labour years from 1997. It was estimated that the Youth Service's financial resources in 1997 had reduced by 11.4% compared to 1986–87. This trend applied to London as well, as Bernard Davies points out:

> *"These downward trends were supported by a London 'mapping report' for 1996 which revealed that, though the lowest reduction for five years, local authority spending on the Service in the capital had fallen by 2 per cent over the previous year and that, to have kept up with inflation since 1991–92, it would have needed to be 15 per cent higher." ('The New Labour Years: A History of the Youth Service in England' Vol 3, Bernard Davies, 2008.)*

In the ensuing years, the Youth Service was subjected to further reductions, as local authorities sought to protect what they perceived to be more crucial services, such as schools and care for the elderly. A survey of local authorities carried out by the Confederation of Heads of Young People's Services in 2011 showed that budget cuts to youth services averaged 28%, but that some authorities were cutting 70% or even, in two cases, all of their services.

New Labour also introduced changes in the way that the Youth Service was funded and delivered, relying on time–limited and short–term funding strategies rather than the traditional and more open–ended grant system. This caused a degree of anxiety to voluntary organisations, which had to adapt quickly to a new regime which focused more on targeting 'socially excluded' groups than on providing a universal service for all young people.

The amalgamation offered some bulwark, however, against these external pressures. Negotiations on this front were completed smoothly, and a new organisation called the Federation of London Youth Clubs came into being on 1 February 1999 to the satisfaction of both organisations, guided wisely by the Federation's unflappable Chair, Richard Sermon, and the Union's thoughtful Chair, Sir David Knox. The immediate challenge for the amalgamated organisation was that it should forge a new and distinctive identity, as Mark Wakefield had anticipated in his final report as the Union's Chief Executive:

> *"It is intended that (the new organisation) will be neither LUYC Mark II nor the Fed Mark II but an organisation that embodies the best of both existing organisations and that builds on our respective strengths to create something new and fresh to respond to the needs of youth work and young people today."*

The new organisation needed also to be promoted to the variety of partners that each had co–operated with as separate organisations. At the end of the first full year of operation, the merged Board expressed its pleasure at the widening profile of London Youth. The Federation's programme of activities continued with little variation, but the London Union's commitment to project–based work was incorporated as a key component of the new organisation's work. Projects begun by the London Union, such as 'Young Women into Safer Surroundings', were brought to a conclusion during this period, and new projects–including the Youth Achievement

Awards–began. The enhanced profile of London Youth as the singular organisation for voluntary youth work across London enabled it to secure funding for the new Millennium Volunteers Project to run for three years from the spring of 2000. The aim of the project was to promote volunteering among young people.

The amalgamation had an immediate effect in easing the financial position of the organisation. Income in the next year was £2,527,758 (an increase of 30% over the previous year) and expenditure £2,479,943, producing a surplus of £47,815 (at today's prices, £68,150). Of the total income, £1,228,667 was donated by trusts and charities (such as the Garfield Weston Foundation, the Joseph Levy Foundation, the Jack Petchey Foundation and the Variety Club), by livery companies (such as the Saddlers, the Girdlers and the Tallow Chandlers) and by business sponsors (such as Deloitte Touche, Byas Mosley and Marshall Amplification). Lever Brothers were an early example of the growing interest of commercial companies in sponsoring the organisation from the 1950s onwards. Its Persil Clean Team Trophy was intended to encourage sportsmanship by making awards to football teams which met certain criteria. Teams were judged on punctuality, the state of their kit, their approach to the game, their attitude to officials and their acceptance of the final result. Government support continued to derive from the Department for Education and Employment (£58,000) and the London Boroughs Grants Committee (£130,000). This positive out–turn gave rise to this note of optimism in the 2000 annual report:

> *"The greater clarity offered by the amalgamation is certainly making it easier for funders and supporters to identify with London Youth's work and its wider mission."*

One note of caution expressed in the annual report was the observation that the surplus was due entirely to restricted funds (funding allocated to a particular project) and not to unrestricted funds (funding that could be used to cover the organisation's overheads, not limited to any specific budget head or project). This constituted the first sign of the impact of the radical shift from a grant-aid system of financial support to a contractual arrangement, whereby charities were commissioned to carry out a specified project.

Under this form of funding, London Youth was able to implement such projects as the Millennium Volunteers and Connexions, which was designed to support young people into work. The involvement of the Devas Club in this work is described in its 2002–03 annual report:

> *"The year's most far–reaching innovation may prove to be the work done at Devas in conjunction with the Connexions Service. One of its detached workers finds the formal atmosphere of the Jobcentre is not ideally suited to the work of confidence–building and developing personal skills. Her task is to provide support for job interviews and preparation of CVs. She thinks the atmosphere at Devas better suited to her methods of working."*

Welcome as this type of funding was, it did continue to present the organisation with a problem in meeting its essential and unavoidable core costs. The 2001 annual report asserted that it remained of the utmost importance to convince future funders of the necessity of supporting the infrastructure of the organisation.

The 2002 annual report reiterated the continuing concern over the difficulty of obtaining funding to cover running costs, in the context of the continuing reduction of Government and local government support of youth services.

London Youth, like the Federation before it, resorted to its perennial solution of an appeal, entitled on this occasion 'My Future'. It was led by Field Marshall the Lord Guthrie (Chief of the Defence Staff from 1997 to 2001), who had become President in 2002 and who brought gravitas to the affairs and deliberations of the new organisation. In many ways, the appeal was meant to address the financial conundrum of generating income to meet running costs. It was intended that, once any revenue shortfall was covered, the remaining money from the appeal would be used to finance a restructure and redevelopment of the organisation's core services and business processes, in the hope that its long–term revenue streams could be improved. The organisation also took steps to review its property portfolio: in 2003, it was able to sell Southfields Youth Club and, after setting up a new, smaller club to replace it, generate a surplus of £563,117; and in 2005 Woodberry Down Boys' Club was sold at auction for £302,000.

The major aspect of London Youth's organisational structure to be reviewed was Club Services. This team had since its inception been seen as a vital element in club development, but the general nature of its work made it difficult to attract specific funds and was therefore mainly dependent for its funding on unrestricted income. The review sought new ways of placing priority on the needs of clubs and concentrating the work of Development Officers on clearly identified need. To that end, a needs analysis was introduced to monitor requests from clubs, matching club visits to the level and frequency of need. Officers also tried to make their interventions more productive by convening area meetings on matters of common concern, so that several clubs benefited from advice and support at the same time. Attempts were also made to encourage affiliated clubs to share resources and give collective consideration to youth work issues.

The financial climate was slow, however, to improve. By 2003, the organisation no longer received a grant from the Department of Education. Though in that year it received a grant of £26,875 from the Association of London Government (which had taken on the financial support given previously by the London Boroughs Grants Committee), this too was discontinued in 2004. Moreover, progress towards the attainment of the appeal's targets had been slower than anticipated. The withdrawal of statutory support meant that London Youth had to seek ways of reining in its expenditure and streamlining its operations. A new organisational structure, introduced in 2005, narrowed down the organisation's focus to four key areas: Member Services, Youth Projects and Interventions, Central Services, and Marketing and Fundraising. This new structure signalled a tighter and stricter approach to financial control:

> *"With the establishment of a new structure and aim that all central expenditure should be fully covered by revenue, an organisational principle has been established that all new projects and posts must be fully funded to include a minimum level of contribution to central running costs."*

Despite these adjustments, however, it continued to prove difficult to ensure that revenue covered running costs (a deficit of £389,611 was reported in the 2005 annual report). The organisation declared its policy of building up its general funds to at least 30% of its annual general expenditure (a target of £600,000) to ensure that its services could continue to be provided in the event of a further deterioration in the level of available funding. It seemed that a degree of retrenchment was the only way to make ends meet. When Joan Howard stood in as Acting Chief Executive in March 2005 on Noel Vallely's resignation, she deployed her business acumen in devising a new strategy, more narrowly based on realising the full potential of the most successful of the organisation's programmes, including the two residential training centres, Activenture (this programme of residential activities at Woodrow High House and Hindleap for young people with disabilities had commenced in 2000) and the Millennium Volunteers project:

"- to build up our affiliation base in order to reach out to the maximum number of London's young people

- to provide premier London training services for youth work

- to expand and improve services provided by the two residential training services

- to continue to provide supported volunteering opportunities to young people in London

- to expand the programme of holidays for young people with special needs"

Within this new strategy, the three major areas of activity were seen to be services to member clubs, courses at the residential centres and special projects.

The circumspection of this period of consolidation did not deter London Youth from developing its residential training centres. Indeed, their success, in financial as well as youth work terms, was perceived to be an indispensable part of the organisation's survival. A major capital appeal for Woodrow High House was announced to develop four, fully accessible bedrooms to increase its capacity to cater for young people with disabilities. Plans were initiated to build a Day Course centre at Hindleap, so that non–residential groups could benefit from its outdoor adventure facilities.

The arrival of a new Chief Executive, Nick Wilkie, in June 2006, marked the emergence of the organisation from its preoccupation with financial challenges. While conscious of the financial uncertainties, Nick Wilkie brought a new clarity and articulacy to the work, restoring ambitious aims and expressing them in a vibrant and uplifting tone, which put a premium on the importance of high quality youth work:

"We want everyone growing up in or around London to enjoy access to high quality youth work with someone to talk to, information and guidance and life-enriching activities, all within a safe, stimulating and supportive environment. Because good youth work works, it helps turn young people into great adults.

We work with young people in all their brilliant diversity, placing a particular emphasis on those who might be in any way disadvantaged or at risk of being excluded."

Youth Action participants on a leadership course at Woodrow High House

The means by which the organisation ensured high quality youth work was, however, beginning to change. The role of those officers variously described as club services officers, field officers or development officers had always been central and undisputed as the most effective way of channelling advice and support to clubs in order to maintain high standards of youth work. But it was becoming increasingly difficult to attract funds for this general role in an era of project–based and time–limited funding. There was also a feeling that it was no longer possible to find the staff who could put the necessary time and effort into forging and maintaining close links with member clubs–or who had the quality and application to emulate previous holders of the job. There was resistance to the elimination of this role, precisely because it had been so integral to the servicing and development of clubs by both the Union and the Federation. Consequently, there was an attempt to identify local sources of funding which could support the developmental role in different areas of London (in 2005, a new Development Officer had been appointed for East London on this basis), but it proved difficult to identify and tap a variety of sources which could add up to a London–wide presence and cover. The organisation instead devoted its energies to putting in place a more structured package of support based upon clubs achieving a set of quality standards. In 2006, a Head of Performance Improvement was appointed to pilot a programme based on Assured Quality for Youth Projects, a model pioneered by Hampshire Youth Options. 35 member clubs were recruited to the first cohort, the scheme was completed by the spring of 2008, and it was planned to spread the programme out to other member clubs from the summer of 2009.

The reinvigoration of the training programme was also pursued as an effective way of raising the standards of youth work within the organisation. By 2007, London Youth was offering training at levels 1 and 2, and for the first time–in collaboration with the College of North London–a level 3 course. 23 youth workers qualified at level 1 (Foundation in Youth Work); 28 at level 2 (Certificate in Youth Work); and 12 were enrolled on level 3 (Diploma in Youth Work). 104 people completed the short Introduction to Youth Work course. A further 98 participated in 18 short courses, including such varied and diverse subjects as conflict resolution, tackling bullying and emergency first aid. As well as providing in-house programmes, the organisation began to provide training for the London Boroughs, which did not always have the resources, in a period of steadily declining funding for the Youth Service, to run their own programmes. In 2007, the London Boroughs of Bexley, Hackney and Wandsworth contracted professional development courses from London Youth. This emerging pattern reversed the state of affairs, prevailing since the post–war inception of a coherent Youth Service nationally and locally, where the voluntary sector looked in the main to the statutory sector to meet its training needs.

New approaches often provoked the complaint from traditionalists that London Youth was losing sight of the Federation's commitment to sports. There was a sense in which the larger, London–wide sporting competitions were becoming less well supported, yet in 2007 1,000 young people took part in the programme of activities and competitions. 80 young people followed the tradition of playing cricket at the annual event at Arundel Castle. New sports, such as street dance, fencing and aerobics, were introduced. Relationships were fostered with national governing bodies, such as the English Table Tennis Association and the England Basketball Association. Partnerships were developed with the Women's Sports Foundation–to encourage increased participation among young women–and with the Prince's Trust–to develop Community Sports Leaders' Awards training for young people looking for employment in sport.

A major development in the sports field was stimulated by the election of London as the location for the 2012 Olympic and Paralympic Games. The implementation of Getting Ready for 2012 and Beyond embodied London Youth's desire to use the profile of London 2012 to arouse the interest of club members in a multiplicity of sporting opportunities and to increase the volume and scope of their own sports programmes. London Youth Rowing was another initiative, launched in June 2004, to open up a new activity to club members. A joint venture with the Royal Albert Docks Trust, the scheme provided week–long rowing camps in the school holidays and supplied indoor rowing machines to clubs for year–round use. In July 2007, London Youth Rowing was incorporated as an independent company, a natural progression for what had become in a very short time an effective and popular project.

The increasing emphasis on project work resulted in the Youth Action initiative. This came out of the Millennium Volunteers programme (which in 2006–07 worked with 600 volunteers whose combined voluntary contribution exceeded 80,000 hours), but was subsequently established as a project in its own right. The project supported young people in taking action on issues of concern to them and in developing their leadership skills in the youth club and local community. A number of 'face the fear' consultations focused on Young Londoners' apprehensions and experiences around terrorism and diversity. As a result of this project, London Youth was asked by the Metropolitan Police to develop its work on diversity. A Diversity Officer was appointed to take this project forward. One example of this work was the production of a DVD by a group of young people, designed to help their peers understand and make use of the Independent Police Complaints Commission.

Another sign of a more ambitious stance was a renewed focus on London Youth's advocacy role, moulded to some extent by Nick Wilkie's public policy background yet also echoing the efforts of earlier generations to shape national legislation. The revamped aims of 2007 included a reference to Voice:

> *"We advocate on behalf of our members, so that the daily experience of on the ground practitioners informs the thinking of powerful policy makers and funders."*

Financial pressures prevented the allocation of significant resources to this aspect of London Youth's perceived role, but there were indications that the organisation was beginning to influence the national debate. Its participation in the Treasury and Cabinet Office Review of Children and Young People resulted in the Government's 10 year Youth Strategy: Aiming High for Young People, perhaps the most forward–looking official pronouncement on the Youth Service for many years. London Youth worked closely with other agencies, including the Partnership for Young London and the Training and Development Agency, to help affiliated clubs better understand the opportunities emerging from Government policy and the new local government commissioning frameworks. It lobbied intensively when the London Boroughs reduced the funding for voluntary youth organisations as they were faced by a wave of budget cuts.

The refocusing of the organisation's activities also led to a review of its governance structure in 2007, overseen in a purposeful and inclusive manner by Davide Rodrigues who became Chair in 2008. The accent was at one level on reduction and streamlining: the number of trustees was reduced from 17 to 12 and the number of sub–committees was limited to three–Finance, Safety and Safeguarding, and Nominations. At another level, the stress was on diversity and skills, so that the Board of Trustees had a more diverse representation reflective of the population of London, possessed the skill sets required to take the organisation forward, and included a more pronounced voice for young people.

The organisation's finances were considerably steadied by the sale of Bridge House in 2007 for £2,885,000. A centrepiece of the centenary appeal, Bridge House had never quite satisfied member clubs as a convenient and appropriate base. Its location in Docklands, too remote for those on the opposite side of the capital and relatively inaccessible by public transport, was unpopular; its warren of rooms did not provide suitable and modern office accommodation; and its wider youth work role as a Training, Arts and Employment Centre, as envisaged in the Centenary Appeal, was never fully harnessed. The trustees agreed that the funds released by the sale (after a new office at 47–49 Pitfield Street in Hoxton had been secured) should be used to provide investment income to ease the pressure on the charity's overhead costs and to fund the maintenance and development of the residential centres. The plan to expand the outdoor education centre at Hindleap resulted in a £2 million scheme to increase the centre's capacity in distinct phases: new dormitory accommodation with 69 beds; refurbishment of the existing dormitories; and a new Day Course facility. Woodrow High House benefited from an extensive maintenance programme, including a major refit of its ground floor accommodation to make it suitable for those with disabilities and to ensure that it remained safe and fit for purpose.

The shift from grant-aid to commissioned provision, with its preoccupation with targets and outcomes, led London Youth to put more effort into attracting funding from external contractors who wished to invest in innovative project work focused on a social concern affecting young people. The impact of the Quality Mark enlisted the support of the City & Guilds, which helped London Youth to explore ways in which it could achieve formal accreditation. (City & Guilds itself was eventually to accredit the Quality Mark in 2008–09.) The louder voice of young people within the organisation's governance structures encouraged the creation of Dare London, a collaboration with the Greater London Authority and the Summer University London. Its role was to ensure that London Youth was relevant and responsive to the needs and concerns of young people. It developed a Young Assessors element of the Quality Mark and advised on the Mayor of London's youth offer. The Youth Works Programme caught the interest of v, the national voluntary charity and the funder of the Millennium Volunteer programme. Youth Works supported groups of young people, who were not in employment, education or training, in volunteering full–time in a youth club and gaining a youth work qualification at level 1. The growing experience of the training section in consultancy work, helping public service providers to deliver programmes to young people, caused Transport for London (TfL) to commission its services. London Youth consulted young people on their experiences of travelling on public transport to assist TfL's youth engagement strategy.

Though London Youth was no longer receiving regular funding from statutory bodies, its vigorous policy of seeking targeted funding from public bodies was reaping its reward. In 2009, it won a major contract to the value of £390,000 from the Department of Children, Schools and Families to launch Positive Change, an anti–gangs initiative, to combat a growing problem of the time. This project, based on five London neighbourhoods, drew together three innovations in a focused scheme of intervention: a specialist anti–gangs initiative, 'Identity', pioneered in Forest Gate; the use of cognitive behavioural therapy in group settings tackling recidivism; and a model of youth action, developing core non–cognitive skills, pioneered by the Keyfund Federation in Newcastle. The organisation also secured funding from the Department of Works and Pensions for the Future Jobs Fund, which created 50 jobs in youth work for long–term unemployed young people. A grant of £97,580 from the Mayor of London's Young Londoners' Fund enabled the organisation to move some of its existing projects into a higher gear, including Getting Ready for 2012 and Beyond (also the recipient of a generous grant from the Girdlers' Company), Youth Action (a scheme which allowed young people to bid for funding to put their ideas into action) and Youth Works.

The reach of these projects was impressive: in 2009–10, 9,144 young people were involved in Getting Ready for 2012 and Beyond, 50% of whom were not previously taking part in sport beyond compulsory PE at school; Youth Works created 130 jobs for young people in long–term unemployment; the Youth Action team worked with 338 young people and trained 164 facilitators; and Positive Change reached 1,105 young people in a range of interventions.

The continuation of these innovative projects, both topical and relevant in the changing context of London life, strengthened the influence of London Youth in its advocacy role. In the wake of the disturbances which took place in London in August 2011, it made a conscious decision to step up its media profile and join in the controversial debate about young people and their involvement in these events. The organisation stressed its view that the press and the wider public should not rush into judgement about the causes of the disturbances. It also emphasised the importance of effective youth work in helping young people to choose positive pathways. The lessons it had gained from its long experience of young people and youth work informed the production of a new book: 'Hunch: A Vision for Youth in Post–austerity Britain'. Sharing ideas and insights from its work in tackling youth violence and gang culture, 'Hunch' posed the question of how policy and programmes could tap the potential of young people's all–round character and capabilities.

These main lines of development were continued by Rosie Ferguson, previously the organisation's Director for London, when she succeeded Nick Wilkie as Chief Executive in April 2012. The London Quality Mark maintained its role of promoting higher standards in youth work practice among member clubs. By August 2012, the award had been made to 72 organisations. The Mark's ability to evolve was proven again in 2012 when it supported Kent and Northumberland Clubs for Young People in developing their quality assurance programmes. The widening appeal of the scheme helped to secure funding from the Department for Education to develop, in partnership with the national body, Clubs for Young People, a quality assurance model for the country–wide youth sector. The growing influence of the training team in supporting clubs was strengthened still further by the introduction of a Continuing Professional Development pilot programme for youth work managers, called Leading Youth Work in a Changing World. City & Guilds backed the programme and supported a research report to distil the learning derived from the programme. The project, Positive Change, maintained a presence in Lambeth to work with young people at risk of becoming involved in criminal activity. Though the contract with the Department of Work and Pensions to support young people into work as part of the Future Jobs Fund came to an end in September 2011, the organisation continued to look for ways amid growing youth unemployment of developing employability skills among young people, including training initiatives and a series of peer–led employability workshops for unemployed young people. The Youth Works programme built on its success in supporting young volunteers, not in education, work or training, in organising their own community projects. The organisation received additional funding from the Mayor's Participation Fund to extend Getting Ready for 2012 and Beyond for a further two years to intensify its work in introducing inactive young people to sports after the initial impact of the Olympics had diminished. A new capital appeal was launched for Woodrow High House to undertake essential preventive and repair work, so that its future viability was safeguarded. £750,000 had been raised by August 2012 to repair the house, grounds and sports centre. Hindleap's enduring reputation was acknowledged by the award of the Gold Standard by the Association of Heads of Outdoor Education Centres.

London Youth continued to prove its adaptability and resilience by devising new projects focused on emerging needs. Urban Nature was an environmental education project, encouraging young people to initiate their own projects based on an environmental theme.

In its first year of operation, 81 members from six clubs attended a residential event to prompt their interest and involvement, and 215 young people became actively involved in developing their environmental initiatives. Megan Pakham, the Director of the Samuel Montagu Youth Centre, traced how the initiative captured the imagination of the centre members:

"The Youth Forum came up with many ideas, but finally decided to keep chickens. The garden was cleared and a chicken coop was constructed. The Forum chose the chickens and set up a rota for feeding them and selling the eggs to the local community. The scheme was later expanded to encompass beekeeping, and hives were built. As a result of these new experiences, the participants deepened their knowledge and awareness about food chains, the importance of pollination and recycling."

Members of Samuel Montagu Youth Club preparing the ground for their project

A new youth action programme, Athan 31, supported 528 young people in running their own projects, so that community action became an integral part of the agenda of youth clubs. London Youth worked in partnership with The Challenge Network (a national charity that supported practical action to strengthen communities) to deliver the National Citizen Service, a new Government scheme for 16 and 17 year olds to take part in social action projects, to 150 young people from Hackney and Tower Hamlets. A new volunteering project, Volunteer it Yourself, enabled young people to gain accredited building and DIY skills by working, under the supervision of local trades people, to fix and refurbish youth clubs in need of repair. This project, in partnership with Wickes and the Co–sponsorship Agency (an organisation which brokered social action projects delivered by public, charity and private agencies working in collaboration) won three awards at the Corporate Engagement Awards in 2012. A Big Lottery Fund grant to March 2014 enabled this approach to be extended across London and the United Kingdom.

The increased focus on project work had led to some degree of detachment from the central organisation among some clubs, principally the long established and more traditional clubs and the smaller, more fragile clubs, which had not become involved in the London Youth Quality Mark, the training offer or the innovative projects themselves. London Youth sought to plug this gap by developing its capacity to support these clubs by launching a new website in March 2011. The new online information pages provided the kind of guidance and resources to help run a youth club effectively and efficiently, addressing issues related to funding, financial management, human resources, public policy, safety and safeguarding, and governance. This approach was designed to give member clubs useful, relevant and accessible information and advice.

This reassertion of the centrality of membership development became a key theme of Rosie Ferguson's bold vision of the future of London Youth, as articulated in the plan for 2013 to 2016. The first of four revised strategic objectives was 'developing, training, connecting and quality assuring our membership network to deliver good youth work'. This objective was to be fulfilled, on the one hand, by the organisation making itself constantly responsive to its members' needs (particularly by capturing insights from the database and the website, by setting up focus groups and carrying out surveys of affiliated groups); and, on the other hand, by encouraging member clubs to learn from each other (particularly in creating specialist networks driven by member need and geared to opening up opportunities to raise income). The other three objectives were:

> *"creating a broad range of opportunities for young people (with and through our members) that improve their all–round confidence, character and skills; ensuring our expertise and the on–the–ground voices of youth workers and young people influence public policy, practice and opinion; being the best we can be ourselves, financially robust and a great place to work."*

These objectives echo the aspirations of the early pioneers of London Youth and affirm the continuity between past and present in the history of the organisation. In many ways, the pioneering role of London Youth's predecessor bodies in the late Nineteenth Century is being reiterated as a key feature of its contribution in the early years of the Twenty–first Century, as the balance between the statutory and voluntary sectors changes under the pressures of reduced funding. This readjustment was reinforced by the tendency of successive governments in this period to regard voluntary organisations as better placed to deliver the new agenda of commissioned and time–limited projects than statutory authorities. In its end note, 'Hunch: A Vision for Youth in Post–austerity Britain' makes a link between the challenges faced by the founding organisers at the birth of the originating bodies in the 1880s and the pressing problems encountered by their successors in 2013:

> "And so, at the dawn of the old century, you could scarcely move, it must have felt, without finding a new institution built for, with and by young people–the scouts, girls' clubs, the flowering of the settlements to name but a few–all emphasising self–government and civic care.
>
> So if, historically, strife has begat strides forward, when this downturn turns up, then, if not before, we need another adolescent spring–a new enlightenment of youth, in which we place confidence less in targets and initiatives and more in character and the reason of rounded individuals."

APPENDIX: Biographies of Key Figures

GEORGE TOURNAY BIDDULPH was born in 1844 in Tunbridge Wells, Kent. His father was the MP for Hereford. He first became involved with St Andrew's Home and Club in 1868, two years after it was founded. Lord Eliot (a diplomat and, later, Liberal MP for Devonport from 1866–1868) had asked him to take an interest in the organisation's activities, and by 1873 Biddulph had become its secretary. For a while, he served as resident superintendent of the Home, supervised the evening club, managed the 'Merry Andrew' (the club's Thames–based boat, which he had purchased and continued to maintain), and organised yearly trips to the countryside. He adopted more democratic styles of government within the club than the more directive methods that were predominant at the time:

> "When club membership started dropping from its original two hundred, George Biddulph regarded it as a sign that his leadership was becoming too autocratic and promptly handed over the management to a committee of boys elected from among themselves." (' A Cry from the Streets', Frank Dawes, 1975.)

In August 1883, he married Lady Wilfreda Palmer, the youngest daughter of the first Earl of Selborne (Lord Chancellor from 1872 to 1874 and again from 1880 to 1885 in William Gladstone's administrations and President of St Andrew's; his great–great–grandson, the fourth Earl, maintains the family's links with the club to this day as one of its Vice–Presidents). The Chronicle, the monthly journal of the Home and Club, concluded its account of the wedding with this tribute to George Biddulph:

> "His life during the last twelve years has been almost wholly and solely for St Andrew's Home and Club, striving in every way to make the lives of its members happy, and helping them by kindly advice, and above all by setting them the example in his own life of how an Englishman should live."

The Chronicle records that Lady Wilfreda Biddulph became actively involved in the life of St Andrew's by organising Sunday classes at the Home.

Biddulph worked as a banker in the family firm of Cocks, Biddulph & Co based at 43 Charing Cross. His career was interspersed with a series of visits abroad–to St Moritz in the winter of 1886, to the Nile and the Holy Land in February 1887, and to Sicily in 1888. A serious illness forced him to leave England to recuperate from October 1884 to May 1885. His return was enthusiastically welcomed by The Chronicle:

> "We have much pleasure in announcing the return of Mr Biddulph who appeared unexpectedly at church on Sunday morning, having arrived in London late on the previous evening. His appearance in the dining room of the Home afterwards was hailed with such hearty cheering as we venture to say has been seldom heard even in that room."

Biddulph withdrew from a regular role in the management of the Home and Club in April 1888, when he decided that he could no longer give 'that attention to the club he desired'. But it is clear that he retained strong links with the club. The Chronicle records that he was a vociferous participant in the debating society's discussion on the role of Trade Unions in January 1894:

"Mr Biddulph thought that Trade Unions have affected some good in the past, but doubted if they were doing any good at present owing to their being ill-advised by the leaders. He instanced several individual cases of hardship caused by the arbitrary actions of the Unions, and did not think that men were free under their sway."

The Chronicle reports that his strong views did not go unchallenged! Biddulph and his wife also extended hospitality to the club at Douglas House, their home in Petersham (now within the London Borough of Richmond upon Thames), where a cricket match between St Andrew's and a Petersham Eleven took place every year. In addition to his association with St Andrew's, Biddulph supported the Scouting movement locally and was the Scoutmaster of the Petersham troop until 1921. Petersham's sea scouts still use a hut on land to the east of Douglas House (the house was bought by the German Government in 1969 for use as a German school).

In June 1893, he was presented with a silver goblet to mark his 25 years of service with St Andrew's. An Old Boy reflected on the impact of his involvement in these comments in The Chronicle:

"What a name to conjure with is that of Mr Biddulph? Who that can remember the years during which a single night's absence from us made us experience a sense of personal loss, can think of anything but gratitude and affection whenever the name is mentioned, and who can wonder at the desire of the boys who enjoyed his friendship, desiring to see once again the man capable of such self-immolation."

Lady Wilfreda Biddulph died in 1910. The 1911 Census shows that George was still living at Douglas House, with a footman, housekeeper, two housemaids and a kitchen maid in attendance. Their son, Victor Roundell George Biddulph, was born in 1897 and was killed in action at the Battle of the Somme in the First World War in 1916, aged 19. George Biddulph retired from the bank in 1919 when it amalgamated with the Bank of Liverpool and Martins Limited. He died on 8 July 1929.

CHARLES WRENCH was born in Surbiton in 1875. At the age of six, he was living with his widowed mother in his grandparents' house in Kingston–upon–Thames. The 1891 Census shows that he was at boarding school at Repton School in Derbyshire. The 1911 Census gives The Bath Club, a gentleman's club in Dover Street in the West End of London, as his residence. The 1912 Electoral Register indicates that he had moved to 17 Victoria Park Square in Bethnal Green, near to the Repton Club, founded by his old school in 1884. He is first mentioned in the Federation's records in September 1908, when–as a representative of the Repton Club–he offered to pay for medals for the winning team at the rifle shooting camp. In December, a sign of his deepening interest in the Federation's affairs, he urged that the monthly circulars should be enlarged and should contain items of news from affiliated clubs. In February 1909, he was offering to book a pitch at the Elms in Walthamstow for the junior football final. He refereed at that time a junior Federation match between St Andrew's Home and Club and St Christopher's. His higher profile led to his temporary election as the Federation's Chairman in October 1909 on Mr Morley's sudden resignation. After Mr Crookes was elected Chairman in October 1910 on a more permanent basis, Charles Wrench took on the dual role of Hon. Secretary and Treasurer.

He was a commanding presence at the Federation during that long period. He fitted in his distinguished service with the Fed with the pursuit of an active business career as a Director of Stevenson Stowell's Ltd, a manufacturing chemist which specialised in essence making. In October 1931, Charles Wrench completed 21 years as Secretary. At an annual gathering in December, in the presence of 1,200 boys representing 120 clubs, Lord Desborough presented him with a gold cigarette case and a cheque with which a radio gramophone set was subsequently purchased. An article in 'Mates', the Fed magazine at that time, had this to say about his arduous responsibilities on all fronts:

> *"Nobody knows whether Mr Wrench spends his 'spare time' managing the business of a well–known firm of manufacturing chemists or the affairs of the Fed. For years, the same premises (1 Bear Lane in Southwark) contained his home, his manufacturing business and the 'Fed' office."*

His hectic schedule did affect his health. In 1922, his doctor ordered him to rest, and he departed to India for a break in his heavy schedule. In March 1923, he 'returned full of beans and good health'. Later, he was again advised by his doctor to take a rest from his work with the Federation.

He was knighted at Buckingham Palace on 10 July 1935. An article in The Times commented: 'quiet, steady, efficient and continual effort has been the hallmark of his work'. The Federation itself paid this tribute to him:

> *"CAW has been almost everything to the Fed for the last 25 years, and only those who are intimately connected with the multifarious details they bring in their train know with what efficiency and modesty he has carried on, often in the most difficult circumstances. In congratulating him, the Committee feel that his well deserved honour is also a public recognition of the work the Fed and its clubs are doing amongst London boys."*

In the same year, he was appointed a Justice of the Peace.

An edition of 'Mates' claimed that Charles Wrench had two vices–golf and going to the pictures. But an examination of the Great Britain Royal Aero Club records reveals that in June 1936 he gained an Aviation Certificate, flying a Gipsy Moth, Gipsy II, 105 h.p. plane, at the London Air Park Flying Club.

He remained Secretary until 1945, and was President from 1945 until his death on 21 September 1948, when he was living in Whitehall Court near the War Office. A memorial service was held at St Martin's in the Fields, and this tribute was paid to him in the annual report of the Crown and Manor Boys' Club:

> *"For longer than any of us can remember, he gave himself wholly body, mind and spirit, to the service of the 'Fed', of London clubs and of London boys. Members of the Crown and Manor, and in earlier days of the Crown Club and of the Hoxton Manor, held him in great affection, as a special friend of their own particular club. He probably meant just as much to the members of every club which knew him."*

His unrivalled commitment lives on in the award of the Sir Charles Wrench Memorial Medallion to those who have given long and meritorious service to the organisation.

CLEMENT ATTLEE became Leader of the Labour Party in 1935, was Deputy Prime Minister during the war and became Prime Minister in 1945 until 1951. He had close links with the boys' club movement through his association with the Haileybury Boys' Club, founded by his old school. Attlee writes of his first visit to the club:

"Haileybury College supported a boys' club in Stepney in the East End of London which had been started by Lionel Curtis, now the distinguished Fellow of All Souls. I thought it would be a good idea to have a look at the club and so one October evening, in 1905, my younger brother and I took a local train from Fenchurch Street Station to Stepney and visited the club. I did not know at that time this was to be a decisive step in my life...(The club) was essentially planned to cater for the needs of boys in a very poor and rough district. Stepney was the home of under-employment and sweated labour. The boys mostly followed blind-alley occupations. Many were van boys. They earned little money but that little was needed to help to keep the family going. By the time they reached the age of eighteen years of age and wanted an adult wage, they were generally thrown out of work with no training for anything...

In 1907 the club manager resigned and asked me if I would take over the job. I agreed, went to live at Haileybury House and thus began a fourteen year residence in East London...There is no better way of getting to know what social conditions are like than in a boys' club. One learns much more of how people in poor circumstances live through ordinary conversation with them than from studying volumes of statistics...

I soon began to learn many things which had hitherto been unrevealed. I found there was a different social code. Thrift, so dear to the middle classes, was not esteemed so highly as generosity. The Christian virtue of charity was practised, not merely preached...I found abundant instances of kindness and much quiet heroism in these mean streets. These people were not poor through their lack of fine qualities. The slums were not filled with the dregs of society. Not only did I have countless lessons in practical economics but there was kindled in me a warmth and affection for these people that has remained with me all my life...I found that in the next street there was a gang of small barefoot boys of school age who had nowhere to go and they asked me if I could do something for them. I arranged to open the club from seven to eight before the senior club opened. Several of the senior boys volunteered to help by keeping order and instructing in boxing and gymnastics. It meant these senior boys snatching a very hasty meal after a long day's work and hurrying to the club. They had no easy task, either, handling these rough little boys, most of them quite handy at throwing stones. But they stuck to their job and it showed, I thought, a good conception of service."

MAUDE STANLEY, like many of the philanthropists who founded boys' clubs, came from an aristocratic background. She was born in 1833, the third daughter of the second Baron Stanley of Alderley. She began her charitable work as a district visitor in the Five Dials area before she became involved in work with young people. She was a prominent supporter of welfare and educational institutions, serving as a Poor Law guardian, a governor of the Borough Polytechnic (now London South Bank University) and manager of the Metropolitan Asylum Board. She was closely associated with Octavia Hill, who campaigned for better housing conditions in the inner city and co–founded the National Trust. She left London soon after the beginning of the First World War, distressed by its outbreak and its impact on life in the capital. She died in July 1915.

In 1890, she wrote 'Clubs for Working Girls', the first significant piece of writing on the subject and a year after T.W.H.Pelham's handbook on working boys' clubs. Again, her motivation was similar to that of her male counterparts in the sense that she was wanting to present upper class values and habits as something to which working class girls could aspire:

> *"If we raise the work girl, if we can make her conscious of her own great*
> *responsibilities both towards God and man, if we can show her that there are*
> *other objects in her life besides that of her gaining her daily bread or getting as*
> *much amusement as possible out of her days, we shall then give her an influence*
> *over her sweetheart, her husband and her sons which will sensibly improve*
> *and raise her generation to be something higher than mere hewers of wood and*
> *drawers of water." ('Clubs for Working Girls', Maude Stanley, 1890.)*

LILY MONTAGU was born in 1873, the daughter of Samuel Montagu, the founder of the banking house of that name. (His successors funded the building of the Samuel Montagu Boys' Club in Kidbrooke, the most expensive and well equipped of the London Federation's 20 Clubs scheme, in 1963.) He entered Parliament in 1884 as a Liberal MP in the new Whitechapel constituency. Her mother was Ellen Cohen, from another family of philanthropists. Lily was the sixth child of ten, growing up in her parents' loving if strict orthodox Jewish home. She left school at 15, but continued to receive private tuition at home until at the age of 17 she began her charitable work. It was the wife of Ramsay MacDonald (the first ever Labour Prime Minister in 1924, the Labour Prime Minister again from 1929 to 1931, and the leader of the National Government from 1931 to 1935) who first introduced her to social work. They later became closely involved in the Women's Industrial Council and the Organisations Committee of the National Council of Women.

When she was 26, she wrote an article, 'The spiritual possibilities of Judaism today', which put forward a new and progressive interpretation of the meaning of Judaism. This prompted the inception of the Liberal Jewish movement in Britain. In 1926, she founded the World Union for Progressive Judaism, adding an international dimension to the movement.

She was the first woman to become a lay minister, and one of the first to become a magistrate in 1920, eventually chairing the juvenile court within the Metropolitan Borough of St Pancras. She was awarded the OBE in 1937.

She died in 1963, and at her memorial service held on 10 February Rabbi Dr Leslie I. Edgar gave this tribute:

"Thus Lily Montagu won for herself a major place in three of the great transformations of modern times. First, the revolution in the place of women in national, and in Jewish, life and service. Secondly, the extending of opportunities to large groups of people who had previously been denied them. Finally, in the development of Judaism, giving a contemporary expression to its age-old ideals."

HARVEY HINDS became the Chief Executive of the Union in 1972 and remained so until 1982. Born into a Worcestershire fruit-growing family in 1920, he won a scholarship to King's School, Worcester. He went on to study at St Edmund Hall, Oxford, subsequently training for the Anglican ministry at Westcott House, Cambridge. A visit to the Charterhouse Mission in Bermondsey convinced him to work in the inner city. From 1944–58, he was assistant missioner at Charterhouse and then became the warden of the Wellington College mission in East Lane, Walworth. He went on to be an honorary canon of Southwark Cathedral in 1969, but had become increasingly frustrated by what he saw to be the Church's lack of desire to change social conditions. This led him to leave the ministry to take up the position of Chief Executive of the Union in 1972.

He pursued a political career alongside his ministry and his youth work. He was elected as a Labour councillor to Southwark Council in 1960 and to the Greater London Council in 1967. He was Chair of the schools committee of the ILEA from 1970 to 1977. His obituary in the Guardian paid this tribute:

> *"His superb organisational and people skills–frequently exercised behind the scenes–came to the fore during the years 1967–83, when he was chief whip of the often volatile Labour group on the GLC."*

Steeped in both the statutory and the voluntary wings of the Youth Service, he epitomised the strength of that partnership. When a commemorative booklet was published in 1990 to mark the London Youth Committee's 50th anniversary, he added this 'very personal recollection':

> *"I refer to the quite astounding generosity with which the LCC/ILEA took on board the admonition of the Board of Education Circular 1486 to local education authorities to 'work in close association with voluntary bodies in full partnership in a common enterprise'. The same message is enshrined in Section 53 of the 1944 Education Act. 'Clear association in a common enterprise' had been the keynote of the LCC Education Committee's approach to the service from the earliest days. The extent to which it happily delegated executive powers to what had been a purely advisory LYC and later to Borough Youth Committees was continued and extended by the ILEA. Nowhere else in the country began to approach this ethos of a 'common enterprise' between statutory and voluntary sides. Not only on the front of grant-aid for all sorts of purposes but even on taking advice from the voluntary sector on the Authority's own direct provision this close co-operation prevailed."*

On the abolition of the GLC in 1986, Harvey Hinds retired to the Hertfordshire village of Trewin, where he created an impressive cottage garden. He died on 1 September 2000 .